Face of Faith

How The Broken Pieces of My Past Turned Into a Magical Life

SHELLEY MAREE

First published by Ultimate World Publishing 2020
Copyright © 2020 Shelley Maree

ISBN

Paperback - 978-1-922714-73-2
Ebook - 978-1-922714-74-9

Shelley Maree has asserted her right under the Copyright, Designs and Patents Act 1988 to be identified as the author of this work. The information in this book is based on the author's experiences and opinions. The publisher specifically disclaims responsibility for any adverse consequences, which may result from use of the information contained herein. Permission to use information has been sought by the author. Any breaches will be rectified in further editions of the book.

All rights reserved. No part of this publication may be reproduced, stored in or introduced into a retrieval system, or transmitted in any form, or by any means (electronic, mechanical, photocopying, recording or otherwise) without the prior written permission of the author. Any person who does any unauthorised act in relation to this publication may be liable to criminal prosecution and civil claims for damages. Enquiries should be made through the publisher.

Cover design: Ultimate World Publishing
Layout and typesetting: Ultimate World Publishing
Editor: Emily Riches
Illustration: Reamolko-Shutterstock.com

Ultimate World Publishing
Diamond Creek,
Victoria Australia 3089
www.writeabook.com.au

TESTIMONIALS

Shelley and I met through an experience that we had in common. We each literally lost our face in car accidents ten years apart, and were confronted with not only years of reconstructive surgery but also reconstructing a life based on something other than the "face" and the identity it represented.

What sets Shelley's story apart is overcoming her back story – one of childhood abandonment and abuse, of drug addiction, and of living in a culture of violence while raising three children, earning qualifications, and coping with years of reconstructive surgery and pain.

In *Face of Faith*, Shelley takes you on a journey from adversity to creating the life she wants, and guides you to overcome your own limiting experiences and self-talk to create the life that you want and deserve.

Kathy Torpie
Author of *Losing Face:*
A Memoir of Lost Identity And Self Discovery

FACE *of* FAITH

Shelley grew up in a survivalist family in what can only be described as shocking. The things she endured would have broken most people. She was not safe or supported by the family unit, forced to grow up prematurely. In an effort to escape abuse, she decided to move to a big city, and by her force of will, breaks through another toxic family situation. Every page has you in disbelief that all this could happen to one person. This memoir and how-to is a story of her internal struggle – to believe in her own version of her life and to have the strength to break away from her past. It gives a glimpse into a way of life that most of us will never know, and it's an inspiring story of one woman's ability to change her future. Read this book now!

Dare to Dream
Kim Stevenson Farmakis
Empowered Eating Coach
Strength Coach
International Level Athlete
Seminar Leader

TESTIMONIALS

Shelley Maree, warrior woman, has given us an exquisitely detailed map of her journey into the experiences that transformed her view forever. Shelley Maree walks hand in hand with the reader as we uncover her trials and tribulations, along with the healing of heart, mind, and body. There is no "sugar coating…" what Shelley Maree reveals is the pure magic she discovered within human nature such as resilience and the power of our thoughts. Such inspiration will be gained by the reader. When reading this book, I thought of the poet Rumi, who reminds us: "is it really so that the one I love is everywhere?"

Rev. R.A. Stewart
B.A Social Science, Monash
Diploma Social Welfare, Monash
Metaphysical Arts Teacher

Everyone has a story to tell, although this one is different to most. If you seek assistance for self-empowerment then this is the book for you. This is about survival and overcoming life's obstacles: mentally, emotionally, and physically, even in the most challenging of times. What's most incredible is with everything Shelley has endured through her journey she has emerged as the most loving, thoughtful and caring person I have ever had the pleasure to know and love. She is standing proof that miracles do happen.

Love you my little elfie ♣
Julie Henshaw
Department of Defence
Public Servant Canberra, ACT

FACE *of* FAITH

What a powerful book. I am deeply touched by Shelley's courage, her love of others, her love of self, and her bright self-awareness for coming all this way. Her journey has been long and difficult. In the first chapters, I could feel her vulnerability and complete innocence. Shelley lived a nightmare as a child and then, just as she settled into life as a mum and a grown woman, a car accident literally tore her face off. Oh my god, I just could not stop reading. I was on the edge of my seat the entire time!

Shelley's guidance on how to begin supporting and helping yourself, as well as how to put it all together in a simple plan, can be applied to anyone's journey. This is a powerful gift for all. Shelley is well on her way to mastering herself. Through all her challenges, her personal growth continued and she never gave up on herself!

I thank her from the deepest part of me for being brave enough to write this book.

To all that are struggling with life in any way, this woman has proved beyond a doubt you can return to your beautiful self where you can connect with the true love residing within your own inner heart.

Sherry Hayden xxxx
Esoteric Healing Practitioner
Universal Medicine Practitioner

TESTIMONIALS

Shelley not only takes the reader on a journey through the many winding and traumatic experiences the human existence can present, but she does it with such insight you feel as though you are with her silently observing and feeling the heartbreaks, the triumphs, and the unknown. Like a phoenix, Shelley has risen from her difficulties and challenges with the steely resolve I remember from when we were 13 years of age: that otherness she seemed to possess. We can adapt, learn, and evolve and that is the human experience. She shows us how to find a different way when we hit roadblocks.

Her dedication to healing and recovery is a guide that can be utilised for anyone who is searching for that "something" and does not feel quite right in their own lives. This is a true guide on how to stop kneecapping your own life.

It is a privilege to know this amazing and courageous woman. Absolutely Inspiring.

Gina Nielsen
Disability Support Worker
Better Health Clinics Australia

Shelley has a powerful story and invites her readers to take the journey with her through experiences and setbacks that would overwhelm many of us. She has come out the other side with grace, living life on her terms, showing that the past shapes us but does not define who we are.

Bronwyn Williams
Founder and Director of Backstory Consultancy

DEDICATION

I spent much time procrastinating over the years, feeling overwhelming fears and blocks every time I thought about finishing the writing of this book. Making the time, finding the mental strength after all I had endured, and the scattering questions – how was I going to be able to go through a publishing and marketing journey and get it out there on my own without any knowledge of how, what, where, and when?

Life has certainly given me a few frightening and death-defying mountains to climb along the way, but I have come out the other side alive and with a gift.

A greater resilience.

A strong sense of self-empowerment.

And a mental strength more powerful that I could ever have imagined!

I dedicate this to my sons, my daughter, my dearest family, and the friends who have become my soul family. I could not have been able to share this beauty without their enduring love and ongoing support, which brought me to a place and ability where I was able to publish this book. There are really no words to describe the powerful gratitude I have for you all on this rollercoaster of craziness we have shared!

I wrote this book for all that have endured trauma of some kind, live with an illness, injury, disability, mental health, or other condition, seen or unseen, in the hope that my words support you on your own healing journey.

Lastly, I thank myself for finding my way here and for the amazing team at Ultimate 48 Hour Author for finding me: thank you for supporting, mentoring, sharing, understanding, and giving me all the extra knowledge and skills to prepare to go through the publishing and marketing process together. My family and this wonderful team all made this possible, enabling me to share my journey, my gift, and against all odds, how I made it to the other side of those mountains and created a magical life. Together, we did it!

CONTENTS

TESTIMONIALS	III
DEDICATION	IX
INTRODUCTION	XV
CHAPTER 1: BORN RESILIENT	1
CHAPTER 2: RAW REAL ADDICTION	21
CHAPTER 3: DYSFUNCTIONAL DEPENDANCIES	33
CHAPTER 4: WHISPERS OF LOVE	47
CHAPTER 5: SOUL SCARS	55
CHAPTER 6: UNRESTRAINED ANARCHY	75
CHAPTER 7: FEAR TO FREEDOM	85
CHAPTER 8: SHIFTING FOCUS	93
CHAPTER 9: MINDFUL MEMOIRS	103
CHAPTER 10: FIND YOUR MAGIC	121
CHAPTER 11: EMPOWER YOURSELF AND TAKE ACTION	141
CHAPTER 12: MIND DYSPLASIA TO MINDFULNESS	173
ABOUT THE AUTHOR	187
ACKNOWLEDGEMENTS	189
THREE BONUS OFFERS	191

I have visited the darkest places

I have been in the deepest depths of despair

I have lived the darkest night of the soul

That is where I found the light

That is where I felt a love so real

There… I witnessed the fairies dance

There… inside my spirit

The Magic happened.

INTRODUCTION

A life lived with love, loss, and hardship

Is a life lived!

A life lived with pain and suffering

Is a life lived!

A life lived with resilience and a courageous heart

Is a life lived!

INTRODUCTION

Miracles really do happen – I lived!

They say cats have nine lives. Well, this human has lived out her nine lives in one lifetime! This was a miracle mixed with, I believe, a certain amount of fate. I say fate meaning the synchronicity of being in the right place at the right time for things to take place as they do.

All things have their purpose in order for us to learn the lesson from the experience we are given. Experiencing life is experiencing growth.

We are all on this amazing life journey, a journey to be shared with others. Understanding this, I want to share my story with you: the trauma I endured, how I healed my mind, my body, and my spirit, to where I am today, how I found the magic in life, in myself, and the things that kept me sane along the way.

At times throughout life we are dealt some challenges. I have certainly lived my fair share of heartache, losses, illness, death, pain, hardships, and broken dreams.

I was born amongst a world of chaos, motorcycle clubs, and bikies, where domestic violence and abuse was the "norm." I was moved from pillar to post, and left the place I came to know as home at 14 years of age.

Later, I worked with people with disabilities, with no real understanding of living with a disability until I ended up on the receiving end of a permanent impairment after a life-threatening car accident. This resulted in my entire facial structure being ripped apart, inside and out. I suffered from a crushed frontal skull, a brain injury, and a permanent disability due to a complex head injury. Following this, I endured ten years of intense bone reconstructive surgical and medical interventions, as well as an infectious bone disease and frontal sinus obliteration.

This was my inspiration to write this book. This affected my entire life, my identity, my mind, my children, and their upbringing. That's the snapshot of the journey that became my path to write, to learn to love myself, and to heal.

All these experiences made me who I am today! I survived it to share this story with you all.

During my journey, I have endured many years of long "incurable illnesses." At times, I felt completely alone, unsupported, and misunderstood, going through many surgeries, medical interventions, and an extended rehabilitation. The lack of support and my grief-stricken heart led me to create my own rehabilitation program, sourcing supports and using alternative healing and therapies that opened my mind and my heart, helping me to heal from the inside out. Weaved through these pages is a mindful approach to rehabilitating the mind, body and spirit. It involves getting back to basics with a more natural "Holistic Recovery Model."

I studied six years in total at various educational institutions across Australia, learning among different fields and from spiritual teachers about how to empower others to help themselves. Before I could share this on a larger scale, the healing had to begin with myself first!

My "learnt through experience" knowledge became invaluable to me while working within the various community sectors. I gained insight and understanding of myself, as well as what I needed and what is needed out there for others, like yourself, who may be enduring similar circumstances.

INTRODUCTION

For those of you who have experienced trauma of some kind, live with a disability, mental health, illness, injury, pain, or other condition; or you have a family member who does; or you may be a carer for someone with one or more of these – I want to share my story with you to inspire you and help you to explore ways to improve your own life, gain better quality of life, learn to love yourself, and find "your magic life." You will be using the tools and strategies I used that helped me to live a healthier and happier life!

Before we continue, I ask you to embrace yourselves for an exciting and, at times, seemingly painful journey ahead. Remember, a life lived with love, loss, and hardship, is a life lived!

Some of the contents of my personal memoir may offend or upset some readers: that is not at all my intention. Keep in mind that these are my own firsthand life events experienced by me which have given me the greatest of life lessons: for that I have grown. I have chosen not to disclose names or any further details to protect those that need protecting. I am not about to apologise for those on the delivering end of what I experienced as my own personal trauma, nor will I apologise for the judgements of a troll's perception. Haters happen when we learn to love ourselves, when we discover our own worth!

Throughout my life's journey I became the "Face of Faith." I discovered magic, I talked to angels, and I danced with fairies, but the life I lived to get there was not G-rated. It was not a sugar-coated fairytale and it is not for the faint-hearted. It is a life lived! It is real, it is raw, it is honest, confronting, and explicit to a degree – just as I encountered the journey. Each and every one of my experiences is what gave me the resilience to bounce back and rise from the deepest depths of despair again and again, feeling more empowered each time. There may be emotional triggers for you throughout and that's ok: it will feel empowering to own those feelings as we work through them, learning to integrate all our experiences and really love ourselves for everything that we are!

CHAPTER 1

BORN RESILIENT

If all the devastation is forgiven...

If all the negatives in life, we look for positives...

If all the broken pieces are put back in their places, no matter what shape...

If each experience we live is learnt from...

If we see the gifts and miracles along the way...

WE CAN AND WE WILL transform our life into a magical one.

BORN RESILIENT

A young man, 18 years old, rolling around the scenes of bikies, gangs, and endless parties in Victoria: this man was to become my father. He worked as a mechanic and fibreglasser, constructing car parts to assemble sports cars in a top quality, high-end Victorian vehicle assembling factory.

My father-to-be met a young 17-year-old girl, barely a woman, with an Indigenous background. This was my mother-to-be. She fell pregnant although she did not want a baby at this stage of her life, having come from an emotionally broken family herself. She had come from generations of a traumatic background: my maternal grandmother was an Aboriginal woman from the Stolen Generation, from which followed a broken childhood, then another broken childhood.

After my birth, there I was, a pure innocent, unaware of the life that was ahead of her, born in the midst of a dysfunctional teenage marriage. Shortly after my mother became pregnant with my sister, she packed up and left, leaving my father and I.

I was around ten months old at the time. I wasn't to meet my sister until many years later. My first recollection of this was when we were eight and nine years old.

My carers became my father, my mother's sister, and the men and women my father associated with at that time.

Around a year later, one night, I was taken by my birth mother from the place my father and I were residing in. It was later confirmed to me, by family, that this act was without consent.

Years later, I was found at four or five years of age in a place for children that had no homes and were made wards of the state. Sometimes, these places were known as orphanages or foster homes; other times, "just lucky enough to have a roof over one's head!"

I spent years in the care of a woman who had a dozen or so other children in her care, who all slept on single dirty foam mattresses with no sheets on the floor of the bedrooms. I remember the toilets had doors that didn't close and there were always children screaming in fear, whilst a man was taking advantage of all the young and vulnerable.

I was one of those children.

These were to be my first recollections of visual memories and frightening fears developing. I had fond feelings for the kind woman who I remember vividly with thick, long, wavy red hair, but felt so afraid for her and myself at this place. I remember hiding under mattresses and locking myself away in the darkest place I could find – inside the wardrobe – so I wouldn't be found. I learnt very young to do whatever I could to protect myself. Not only were the children being violated and abused, so was this caring woman.

I later found out this was, in fact, a foster place for orphan children and I was dropped off there after I was taken from my father's residence as a baby.

Soon after discovering my whereabouts, my paternal grandfather (my father's father) had filed paperwork and fought the system, trying to win back their family rights to me and the rights of my upbringing.

Later, he won the rights over my upbringing and I was collected from this "roof over my head" foster place and taken to their farm.

BORN RESILIENT

I stayed with my grandparents for the next four to five years. Those years were spent getting to know my biological family: my nanna, my father, his partner, aunties, uncles, cousins and the like, who were all (in the early stages of that first year with them) strangers to me.

I felt alone and still so afraid at times, as there were so many people that I did not know or feel comfortable with. These people I was calling Dad, Nan, Pa, Aunty, and Uncle, I had no memory of as a baby before I was taken away. I still found myself hiding in dark places, under beds, in cupboards, and in the daytime, hiding in the neighbour's acres of overgrown fruit and vegetable crops. The strawberries were delicious!

I would have sleepovers and family holidays where I would meet and spend time getting to know my father and his partner and the extended family over time. Although, for a long time, I felt outside of the family, not really a part of the tribe as I had not been for those early years of natural bonding.

I was, at times, a neglected child, rejected and starved of life's basic needs. This was a totally "normal" way of life for me and something I was not to understand any differently until my early adult years. There were many factors and influences that impacted my wellbeing and affected my growth.

Those years residing with my paternal grandparents were spent helping out on my grandparent's small farm. There were dogs, cats, chooks, lambs, and my first horses my father had given to me.

FACE of FAITH

BORN RESILIENT

I loved playing with and taking care of the animals. The gardens were amazing too. I learnt a lot about gardening and how to grow vegetables and various plants which my grandfather would sell at his regular market stall. He sold all kinds of things from homemade jams and furnishings to second-hand items. I was lucky enough to be shown these skills from this young age.

Learning to grow plants, make crafts, and create and build things with my own hands gave me a great sense of achievement. I enjoyed being busy: doing, working, or creating. It was therapeutic to do what I love and still is.

My nanna suffered with illness and was unable to communicate effectively. She had a major speech impairment and was unable to care for herself independently, having endured her first severe stroke at 21 years of age and continuing to have countless strokes throughout her life, deteriorating with each one. We lost count after 13 strokes. As minor or major as they were, as each one took place, they damaged her brain and she became more dysfunctional and childlike as time passed. She needed assistance and care with the majority of day-to-day basics. But nothing stopped her wandering off on foot around the town or finding the keys to her car and taking a drive to buy groceries and cigarettes. I swear she lived just to smoke her pack of cigarettes a day! Luckily, in the small country town where we lived, almost everyone knew us and knew of her condition. They would give her what she wanted for the 50 cents she would give them in return for all the items, then send her home for her own safety. My grandfather always had an extraordinary grocery account to be paid.

God help us all if we left the shampoo or dishwashing liquid out where she could find out – she drank it a few times, bubbles galore. My grandfather had to install a stove outside under a corrugated iron roof because she loved to cook but it was a disaster every time. I mean, we are talking rice, pasta, jelly crystals, custard powder, chocolate, or whatever she tipped into a pot. It would harden to charcoal unless we turned it off in time! It was trial and error for me also, I didn't know the first thing about cooking. After many arguments, she came to understand her stove was outside and she would go out there and cook until the dog's stew was charcoal. She was very proud of her achievements, and poor little Timmy had to eat what he was given.

I had to think for both of us at times and if I forgot, look out. There was a never a dull day living under the same roof as my nan!

Caring for Nan and assisting with day-to-day basics was a huge part of my own daily life. I spent more time at home with her than I did at school. I spent some part of the time looking for her when she got the wanders up and some part of the time hiding from her because she would lose the plot completely, clapping her hands and shaking her fists ferociously, stomping her feet abruptly, then running around the house making strange and angry noises which sounded like, "Quick quick quick." She'd give me a look of, "I am about to murder you," and even the dog would come running and hide with me. Apparently, everyone would clear the pathway for kilometres when my nan expressed her anger! I would sneak back to the neighbour's acres of fruit and vegetables. I ate strawberries for hours at a time until I couldn't hear any more noises coming from the house.

It was easier to distance myself and find something to do that I enjoyed. It was a way I cared for myself without realising it at the time.

I grew a lovely close connection, like a mother-daughter bond, with my nan, even though she had a terrible sickness, was not completely sane, and I took the caring role in the relationship. She became like a mother to me in the way I felt about her!

I had a playmate in her: one who giggled as much as I did and could be so naughty. She was always getting in trouble. We kept many secrets, swearing not to tell my grandfather the things we got up to. I'm not sure she ever really understood my secrets, but I cleaned up and hid a few of her natural disasters, and never told a soul to try and protect her from the carnage when my grandfather got home. I knew she didn't understand, as she was younger mentally than I was.

Over those years, she grew sicker and continued to have strokes. I found myself caring for her and becoming the responsible carer from an early age, while my grandfather worked two jobs. He grew all our fruits and vegetables, jarred, preserved, or dried everything he grew, and built furniture in his spare time to sell at his market stall. My grandfather was a hardworking man.

Our weekends were dedicated to his market missions, my piano lessons, and going to church and Sunday school with my nan. Then we would drive three hours to meet at these spiritual, psychic gatherings. This was where I discovered my love of music, Buddhism, Shamanism, and other ancient scriptures and teachings from around the world. These group gatherings gave me the insight and understanding to face the experiences on my life's journey so far and what was ahead of me.

My grandfather also gave me a great gift: teaching me to read and write quite well before I went to school. I still love to write.

They were the great things my grandfather did and everyone said how much he loved me. But he loved me a little too much.

Sadly, he was another of the men I encountered through my childhood years who had an attraction towards me. He did unwanted and overtly affectionate, sexual things to me against my will, that I did not like. I harboured this secret with guilt and shame for many years to come. This was the first man I had believed in and he had shattered this new developing trust in my heart. I found myself taking off and hiding in all kinds of places. The cemetery up the road was one place I spent a lot of time, escaping the painful reality of my situation.

After spending these years in the care of my grandparents, at nine years of age I moved in with my father, moving about a few times.

My father was also a hardworking man: as well as constructing sports cars from the bottom up, he had a horse-riding school for a while with many horses and other animals. Alongside his hard work, he played hard too. He was not around much of the time with work and social engagements. When he was around, he was busy working and training horses. Nevertheless, I learnt to trust him and we formed a close relationship and lovely friendship over time. He was always a "happy-go-lucky" person and kind to me. However, others residing with us at the time were not.

I was born in a wild time and for the rest of my upbringing, I grew up around the bikie scene: clubhouses, rock'n'roll, wild parties and even wilder hangovers, the smell of alcohol and burning rubber, men being meatheads, arm wrestling and, at times, sparring until there were panes of glass broken and everyone involved had bled what resembled a crime scene.

It was frightening to see time and time again, to say the least! I witnessed socially underdeveloped men who abused life and the system as much as they did their women, with those women believing it was ok and "normal." Some spent their lives with bitter resentment, and even took it out on their children.

There were others residing with us at different times. Some were kind and some not so kind. The not so kind ones endlessly degraded every aspect of who I was, physically and mentally abusing my young, vulnerable mind and body. I clearly remember being repeatedly told I was ugly, called the cruellest of names, screamed at, and physically attacked with bridles, lead ropes, the girths off saddles, and the whole saddle itself if I was close enough to have it launched upon me. This left me with welts, bruises, and a shattered self-esteem. I never felt good enough or worthy of kindness. Hell, I ended up getting belted and excluded from fun rock'n'roll card games nights, just for dancing around the lounge room with all the usual suspects that came regularly!

A few years prior, whilst residing with my grandparents, I was diagnosed with an enlarged bowel and Irritable Bowel Syndrome Disorder. This was horrendous and an extremely painful medical problem I endured for many years. This disorder required a major surgical procedure in order to treat it which, I recall, was discussed multiple times. However, the end result of these discussions was just to leave it untreated. Due to this ongoing serious condition, it at times left me with complete loss of control of my bowels. This went on for many years until I left home, attended the doctors, and finally received medical treatment required to relieve this excruciatingly painful disorder.

On many occasions, when family or friends come to visit, they would get a tour through my room to find my days-old dirty clothes and underwear hanging from my wardrobe handles, doorknobs, and hooks around my bedroom, or hanging on all the laundry hooks and knobs if I had not done my laundry. I was repeatedly shamed for having such filthy clothes and told how ugly and horrible I was in front of our visitors! On some occasions, I was told to stay in the bedroom and scrub my walls to make it clean until others had left, only occasionally allowed to engage with family and friends who came to visit.

Again, this became "normal" to me at the time. I was nine years of age, and did not think to question the behaviour of the adults I resided with. I became so frightened that I would not dare speak out loud anything I was thinking around these people. Even so much as expressing an opinion on something caused a crazy and violent reaction.

This kind of shameful humiliation, emotional bullying, intimidation, and violence I endured from such a young age pushed me to a place deep inside myself. It impacted my ability to learn, to grow, and to experience any form of love for myself or others for many years of my life.

I was questioned and bullied at school when I turned up with welts and bruises, and for not being able to control my medical disorder at times. I was a mess, with a cramping belly full of worms and a head full of lice and scabs from the constant scratching. It makes me itchy remembering it! It hurt so much for many years. I couldn't brush my hair too often as my scalp would bleed, and the only relief I could get was to run hot water over my scalp, as hot as I could handle it. I would scream out loud from the pain.

Some years later, a school nurse began speaking with those that took care of me about some of these issues. This nurse even asked me over for sleepovers at her home and treated me with all sorts of tablets, creams, and concoctions.

I went to school only occasionally. It depended if I could get a lift off anyone that was around or if I had washed my laundry and had clean clothes to wear. Once I hit high school and we moved to the country, it was around a 1.5 km walk to the end of the driveway where the bus would pick a few of us up.

Either way, there was no home-baked cookies, bedtime stories, packed school lunches, neatly folded washing, tutoring, or sporting activities for this kid. Those things were privileges and luxuries that I only witnessed in other families. At the time, I did not understand those basic things we have a right to.

I was totally blown away and amazed at how other families lived and the things they had and the way they spoke to each other. It was strange for me. I absorbed as much kindness as I could take in during sleepovers with friends. It was a privilege.

Spending this time growing up around these types of behaviours meant that they all became my "normal." This set the standards for my growing belief system and what I would put up with for years to come.

But why? Why would I put up with being treated this way? This "normal" behaviour and lifestyle that I became accustomed to was to become my life and the types of relationships I would put up with. How would I have grown up believing or thinking any different, when I did not experience or witness any different?

During these years I spent with my father, I found something else to focus on, something I grew to love. I developed a deep love for animals: horses in particular.

We were long distance endurance riders. We had camping adventures every few weeks with these beautiful animals. I never came first in an endurance ride, but got a few seconds and thirds and the prize for best-conditioned and best-behaved horse were my specialty trophies. My dad always said there wasn't a horse feral enough that I could not tame, even if I did hold the reins between my teeth at times when the horse's behaviour was relentless and my hands couldn't take anymore! People thought he was crazy giving me the lunatics to ride, but it taught me to hold on tight, learn to read their problems, and listen to their whispers. Once they would quieten down, I would get bored and soon be looking for another challenge.

I never went much for horsey people's "how to" advice, as each horse had their own breeding, personality, journey, needs, habits, and fears that all shone through their language. I learnt to feel my way by listening to their whispers to work with them. Much like humans, horses also need to be listened to in order to feel understood, and to have their needs met.

BORN RESILIENT

There was always a rescue animal on our doorstep needing TLC and I was the vet nurse (at least I thought I was)! My father was no vet, but he certainly knew how to treat every problem a horse had.

I learnt everything I could possibly learn about horses from all the knowledge my father shared. I buried myself in daily horse rides, riding far and wide, anywhere and everywhere, and spent many hours every day training and caring for the horses. I grew a strong connection and love for these beautiful animals. It helped me escape the hostile violence that erupted regularly.

Training and caring for horses became my entire world for a big part of my upbringing. My world revolved around them. Although we owned a lot of horses, I didn't consider myself a "horsey person," as they were highly competitive "know-it-alls," that looked down on me because I didn't wear the fancy pants, velvet helmet, or a rodeo buckle. I knew nothing of the inside of a dressage arena and the furthest thing from a rodeo queen or a pony club show jumper. Our horses were not show horses by any means and I didn't own a hat of any sort. I just loved being around them, listening to their needs, and training them. I found an affinity, a serenity, and healing working with them. They almost became a part of me, something I could not live without. They became my daily dose of therapy amidst the chaos and emotional trauma.

Working with these animals took me to another place, away from all the emotional torment I had felt. I found a confidence and trust in them that I had lost in humans. This became my positive, my light in the midst of all the dark. Daily training gave me the ability to ride it out – ride out all of what had happened and was happening in my life.

I not only found my love and connection with horses but with nature too, living on a large property amongst bush and pretty landscapes.

We lived in a large unlined shed. The roof was lined with cardboard, a breeding ground for big, dirty huntsman spiders that would come out at night and run down the walls into our sleeping areas and crawl along the beds. I always slept with my head as far under the covers with no gaps to let any of those frightening creatures inside my safe haven. I still have a phobia of those disgusting things! Inside the shed, it was partly a dirt floor. Some sections were concreted with old carpet pieces for coverings. We boiled bucketed water from our dam and cooked meals on our 44-gallon bricked-out drum, the hot water buckets filled the bath tub for us all to bathe at the end of the day. Later, we installed a fibreglass shower and a header tank on the roof with a pump at the dam to pump water to the tank. Then we only needed to chop wood to light the Donkey to heat the water before we showered in our carp-filled dam water. That made the nights a whole lot easier!

Our luxury lifestyle shed had no electricity, but we did have generators: one to run lights and one to run heavier items when needed, such as the old crank-winding wringer roller washing machine to wash the clothes. For this, we had to crank the winder to feed the clothes through the wringer. My winter woollen-pleated high school skirt did not like being squashed into the roller, and came out looking worse than when it went in! Then I would heat up the old iron on the 44 drum to iron the creases out of my skirt. The generator didn't like the electrical iron. We did not have a toilet but my father dug huge holes deep into the ground and put a row of "floorboards" built out of a timber crate and a rusty old pit toilet over the crate. This was inside an old, rickety, falling-apart tin shed. All I know is the door did not close properly and the whole thing felt like it was going to fall over. We had to lean to one side while seated, so it wouldn't fall over. When friends would visit, most would never return. It was a bit of a shock to some, leaving them speechless as to how luxurious our lifestyle was... haha! Again, it was normal for me!

By 11 or 12 years of age, I think I gained the title of the youngest, hardest-working human ever, with the daily running of the property, training horses, and slashing acres of bracken fern paddocks with a hand slasher for hours at a time. I was dreaming, sleeping, and inhaling bracken fern.

I worked with my father completing fibreglass jobs when he had a lot on. He paid me well, $4 a day (if I did everything required) and picked up some weekend work here and there at the local carrot farm, picking and bagging carrots, earning extra cash to buy all my own toiletries, clothes, shoes, and school-wear, or whatever I needed for myself.

My sister had been sent to live with us. We had met in recent years, had a few visits, and developed a beautiful friendship. Although I think our luxurious lifestyle – the hard work, hectic horse training schedule, and frightening acts of abusive violence towards us – took some adjusting to. Two years or so later, my sister was moved again. We were both devastated.

By 13 years of age, I was failing school. School was really at the bottom of my 101 things to do each day. The daily task list grew longer and more tedious with dogs having puppies, more animals to care for, and a few further property developments to help with. I had developed pneumonia for 12 months or more but was still horse riding six to 20 km a day in the rain. Our motto was to train, rain, hail, or shine!

My father had employed numerous young men to assist with the property and business, one of whom used to get drunk and sleepover on the lounge, across from my bed. On more than one occasion he sexually took advantage of me, until I told my father what was happening. That was the end of that.

Soon after, my grandfather passed away after suffering cancer. When he died, so did the shameful and guilt-ridden secrets I kept for many years to come.

This was the first time I experienced depression firsthand.

I sprained my ankle but kept using it as normal for months until it became so swollen and painful, I just could not walk. Doing everything to "help others" was ingrained in me, and I had not learnt what it meant to take care of myself! Without support or anyone I could talk to, I mentally began to fall apart. I began staying in town with friends much older than myself. I began dabbling in all the drugs and alcohol offered. I developed a drug problem. I did not want to feel the way I was feeling any longer. Self-medicating became my escape mechanism. It certainly took me away from the painful reality of what my life was at the time. I met a man who I was to have my first real relationship with. I could see a man that was also in need of help and took it upon myself to try to help him, as I had previously learnt it was my job to help everyone around me. I also had learnt not to judge a book by its cover: all I had seen was a good man with some behavioural problems. Just like the type of men I grew up around: men that other men feared and women ended up frightened of. I became comfortable with what I was afraid of, as that's what I was familiar with.

BORN RESILIENT

My home lifestyle taught me to be fiercely independent and take care of everything else and others needs at the expense of myself – a belief I was to battle with for a long time into the future!

At this point, my tribe now felt like my family. I knew everyone well, although I didn't feel I had a place to call home. I felt an urge to pack a bag with the few things I owned and venture out into an unknown world. I booked a bus ticket to the other side of the country to a city to search for my maternal side of the family.

CHAPTER 2

RAW REAL ADDICTION

Ask those who do not know

And they will have you follow

A path of painful sacrifice

Of darkness and all things not nice.

RAW REAL ADDICTION

Now I had removed myself from soul-disturbing situations, I was off on another journey, adventuring to an unknown land in search of family that were mine, yet nevertheless, were strangers to me.

The only contact I had previously had with my mother was a meeting at a train station and two recent short holidays with her while she was staying close by. I was 13 years of age at the time. I did not know her well or know much of her. I only knew what I witnessed and the photos I kept from those two holidays. Interesting photos they were, of me dressed in all kinds of tiny, skimpy tops and skirts with a little lace here and there, almost naked. In some, I may as well have been! My mother had talked of me becoming a model of some kind. That could be exciting. Surely my mother would help me see my way clear of the foggy road I had been on – she brought me into this world after all.

I was now 14 years of age. I had a bag of flannelette shirts, jeans, my riding boots, a pair of thongs on my feet, and $50 my father gave me as he dropped me off at the bus station. This lasted me the three-day bus ride across the desert, and I was heading to a huge city! This was the last time I would see my father for the years I was there.

I was "jumping out of my skin" excited! I went walkabout in search of a family that were mine to meet with for the first time that I remembered.

At the time I thought, "These people will love me, they will be proud of me." I was independent, I did housework, I worked really hard, I was a great horse trainer, I knew how to take care of animals and was great at it. I could get a job and pay my own way. I was used to working and supporting myself. I lived just to please all the people and animals around me. Surely this family would appreciate what I had to offer.

Although the last year of my life had taken a dark turn, I was away from all of that now and planning a great future in my head. At this point, I just wanted to bond with them and get to know a family that I had not had the opportunity to know. Yet my naivety and lack of awareness of addiction had remained. At this point, I had no idea what I was in for over the next three years.

Within less than a month of arriving in this unknown "big city," on the other side of the country that was many states from the shed I once called home, I found myself homeless, with not a cent to my name. I desperately needed to find a doctor, but I had no documents to identify my identity, no birth certificate to prove my existence, no Medicare number, no social security number, and no-one to help me figure out what I could do from here. I knew my name, age, date of birth, and had packed my school reports, school photos, and bank account that was opened when I was in primary school in my "leaving home" bag. Those were all I had that were mine! My childhood bank-book and school photos and reports with my name on them was enough for the police to do a statutory declaration to declare my identity. Then I was able to obtain a Medicare number and my very own card with my name on it. I was unable to claim any government benefit until I had obtained a birth certificate. I found a post office and asked for help. I obtained an application for a birth certificate and asked them to make copies of every school photo, report, and form of identification I now had, including my new statutory declaration and Medicare card. I posted this along with my application. The lady at the desk helped me fill it all in and even paid for my envelope and postage for me. I was ever so grateful.

RAW REAL ADDICTION

I discovered quickly that the mother and family I had longed for had their own difficulties and lives to deal with. I was a teenage stranger to them, another mouth to feed, and was not welcomed in the way I had imagined. Other family I met offered me a bed or a lounge for a week. Some offered longer than a week.

Some of the kinder family members helped make appointments and showed me around to where I could get food from charities and where to catch buses. The boyfriend I had before leaving caught a plane across to visit me within weeks of my arrival to discover I had nowhere to live. He decided to stay, but now we both had nowhere to live!

Within three months of my arrival, my birth certificate arrived. I applied for Young Homeless Allowance and joined an employment assistance program. I applied for a tiny short-term holiday caravan to rent in a small seaside village caravan park, explaining my homelessness and lack of money. They were kind enough to accept even though neither of us had any cash until both our payments came through. We moved in. I was not bothered by having no money, as I had a roof over my head. I was ecstatic!

That was to be the first of many places we resided in for the next three years.

During the process of finding my feet, I lost them just as quick. I was already familiar with drugs, and concoctions of speed and pills within the circle I associated with before I moved away. What I was about to embark on was an even bigger shock to my system than anything I had ever experienced.

A family member I looked up to and her friends introduced me to a heroin-fuelled lifestyle. I quickly became addicted and experienced a sickness that ran through every cell in my body.

With this heroin lifestyle came a life of crime and being taught to dance beautifully with seductive clothing on. I had no idea at the time that I was being groomed for what they thought was going to be their future income. These influences were thickening the fog that I was trying to see my way clear of.

"Follow me, I will show you a life of heroin, crime, pain, and manipulation," was all I could hear from those I looked up to. I was being given large doses of drugs for free. They had no problem wrapping a tourniquet around my arm and administering heroin as though it were a daily medicine as I did not know how to do this myself. In fact, if I didn't allow this, I would become horrendously ill, vomiting non-stop until I thought I was going to die. This continued for the next 12 months.

The night before I turned sweet 16 was like an initiation night for me and a celebration for those who were awaiting my legal coming of age. I had no idea at the time what was happening this night, but I sure looked pretty. I was dressed up in an all-white leather mini skirt, jacket, and heels, done up to look like a much older woman. A much older man led me in and later was to lead my boyfriend away to the gambling areas. This was going to be a night of fun. I walked down an elegant hall into what seemed a gold-lined palace – to me it was! This place was known as The Hilton. I discovered it was a nightclub casino for dirty, rich old men who preyed on young, vulnerable, and drug-addicted girls who, like myself, were not even women yet. I was being introduced to an assortment of gentlemen who were very kind to buy me cocktail after cocktail.

The family member and friends who accompanied me on this night gave me more of the daily medicine that helped me relax. They told me to go dance on this small platform area among a corner lounge. Other girls around my age were dancing alongside me. Sometime later they called me over and said I had danced beautifully and they had a financial surprise for me. They had explained to me I was now of age to perform the duties requested by a man that just paid them $1,000 for my dance and another $1,000 to buy me for the night and I would get my share!

I had just realised what this was about. I explained to them I would never prostitute myself or give my body to anyone. I could not do anything like that and I had no idea they were being paid for me to dance. I just thought we were coming out for my 16th! It was then explained to me that now I was of the age to make my own money and I had to pay for all the drugs I had been given. I would be getting less than 50% of what I made; they offered me $1,000 out of the $2,000, but only when I got picked up in the morning.

I felt devastated and frightened. I began crying, arguing, screaming, and refused to do what was asked by this family member. I was grabbed aggressively. They were holding me tight and told me that this was business, I was not able to stay a child forever. I would do as I was told, as this was the way things were done. They would not put up with any teenage tantrums and I was becoming an embarrassment to them and their business! They became really angry, and arguments and upset escalated between a few in the group whilst I was still being held.

At that moment, I realised I was never going to get their love or approval because they wanted something from me that I was not going to give. I was shattered that this family member would sell my body for money to feed their own addictions and the addiction that I now had.

I had to act fast or I was going to be forced into a worse situation than I was already in. I had just turned 16 years old and quickly learnt the meaning of self-preservation: to do what you need to do to protect yourself. I planned quickly.

I apologised for the drama and embarrassment I had caused them, said they could keep all the money made on this occasion, and excused myself to go tidy myself up in the bathroom for a long night ahead.

In fact, I ran right past the bathroom. I ran as fast as I could out those doors that night, leaving my boyfriend behind in the gaming room. One of the people in the group chased me, but I kept running down city streets and alleys, through parks lit with only the dim light of street lights.

Once I couldn't hear anyone chasing me, I hid underneath large overgrown hedges that backed up to the cyclone fence of an alleyway in the dark. The ground was damp and the hedge I lay under was dripping water over me. My hair was soaked, as was my white mini outfit. I had not even been aware that it was raining until I stopped running and climbed under the bushes. I had no money, and was not sure where I was or how I was going to get back to where I lived. I felt frightened, tired, and cold after a while. Not that I cared. I was safe and that's all that mattered to me right at that point!

I also felt something else. I felt a sense of empowerment. I realised now that I had been groomed for the last couple of years, beginning with the near-naked "modelling" photos that were taken when I was 13 years of age. I just made a choice that was right for me, and, as frightening as it was, I followed through with that decision and took care of myself.

I thought about many things that night whilst the sickness set in. I did not want a life like the one they had introduced me to. Once I felt calm, I slept the rest of the night until it was daylight. I lay there until the sun came up, on a bed of damp old debris and fallen leaves under the bushes.

I was so very sick. I could not stop vomiting. I walked for hours until I found a street name I knew, following familiar roads that took me back to where I was residing at the time. I got over being groomed into a shape that didn't fit or feel good for me at all.

The family member and others turned up that afternoon, upset with me, there was an exchange of hurtful words for not doing what was asked and anguish caused but nevertheless gave me sweet 16 birthday flowers, a gift, and drugs. It was my birthday, I had almost forgotten!

I took a full-time job at a food outlet after this to pay for my habit, distancing myself from all these people. A number of these people went to jail for terrible crimes they committed. Crime was never something I was ever interested in. I learnt from a young age that you worked hard for your money!

It saddened me deeply to witness toddlers being neglected, some becoming motherless and fatherless as their families fell apart, all due to the use of drugs.

Just after I turned 17, I attended the counsellor's office and medical centre, telling my life story. I had made the decision to overcome this dreadful addiction. What ignited my drive behind this decision was that a week before my birthday, I spent a night held in the city lock-up. I was in a backroom with a lady police officer who bought me dinner, gave me a couch to sleep on, and bought me back to reality with her kind words and referrals to services to help me. Instead of arresting me, this officer spent all hours of the entire night unpacking the reasons I had taken this path after she realised I had no real support or legal guardians. She offered her help in finding people who could help me, if I would help myself.

I made a promise to her and to myself that I was going to overcome this addiction. I had to: it was either that, or death, in the long run.

She dropped me home the next afternoon after making many appointments and gave me a bus card to travel to and from these appointments.

I attended each and every appointment she made for me. This officer put me on the path to wellness. I had hope that I could be normal again!

That became a huge battle but it was a battle I conquered through community support programs, health and wellbeing courses, counselling, dietary help from a dietician, and home self-rehabilitation. I was terribly sick for many months, suffering hallucinations and terrible nightmares. The vomiting, sweating, and shaking eased off after two months. It was a long two months though, I tell you! I had to quit my job because I could not stop vomiting. I had learnt the use, abuse, and debilitating journey of this type of addiction. Throughout my recovery, I continued to attend the community support programs.

Overcoming this felt like death, a cellular sickness, that took time for my body to expel all the toxins.

This was the beginning of my turning point: my first steps moving forward, to rehabilitation, and discovering what I really wanted to do with my life. What could I create for myself?

RAW REAL ADDICTION

I began goal-setting and planning what I wanted for my future. I had plans and goals to achieve, once I was well enough!

I had planned on having a baby, moving back to Victoria, enrolling in an education institution, and renting a nice house. I did exactly that!

As the months passed, it eased a little. Some days, long enough to start long walks which turned into running. I found it therapeutic to run. After eight months had passed, I felt fitter and healthier than I had ever felt.

Then the new discovery, this tiny seed, the size of a pea: a new life, growing inside my belly. The day I found out I was six weeks pregnant changed my entire existence forever. It was a miracle!

I still wasn't completely out of the woods and had a lot of sickness, but I felt blessed.

This pregnancy led me to the discovery of a new teenage girl coming into bloom, the birth of this beautiful life that made me so happy and kept me drug-free! I owed this gift a world of love and promise!

CHAPTER 3
DYSFUNCTIONAL DEPENDANCIES

Where there is no love,

There is no guiding light,

With nurture, I became a beacon of

Compassion that shone bright,

As I carried this inevitable storm

Hail burnt my fingertips,

Miracles of love were born,

An unspoken silence fell on my lips,

FACE of FAITH

A painful circle, a chapter untold

With truth on my side,

In time would unfold,

To make a difference, to guide

Leaving lessons learnt and miracles behind.

DYSFUNCTIONAL DEPENDANCIES

My body bloomed with this growing love I felt. I wanted to be the best mother I could be. I wanted to give this child the best life possible and all the love I never had! For me, this meant going back to Victoria, finding stability, and a comfortable home to live in.

We began planning the return trip and spent a few months staying with my partner's family, who opened their home and hearts to our homecoming. We stayed with them for the time it took to get on our feet and move into a comfortable home before the arrival of our child. I felt blessed to have spent the time I did at their home. My partner's mother was the mother hen I needed who wrapped her wings around me becoming like a mother to me. She gave me many cooking lessons, driving lessons, and lessons on how to remain sane even when I felt I wasn't!

Yearning for knowledge, I did pre-natal classes, booked into parenting courses, read baby books, parenting books, and as many health, wellbeing, self-love, and self-help books as I could find at local libraries. My lack of education and hunger for it gave me the drive to learn how to be a positive parent, how to cook a variety of dishes from around the world, how to be fit and healthy, and how to live a family life. After 17 years of unhealthy behavioural patterns, injustices, and a lack of love, not only in my life but in myself! Not knowing any different other than what I had experienced, I wanted to make it all right inside and outside of myself.

I was now growing!

Once I had passed the initiation into adulthood, turning 18 years of age, some of my old friends I had caught up with were having a long break from their education and heading out to explore the world of partying. I had already experienced enough of that world and was almost ready to go back to school. My world, for now, revolved around setting up our home and my baby's nursery, getting creative, making and painting a few pieces of furniture – the skill I had the opportunity to learn early in life.

My first child was nearing. I had remained free from addiction, and continued that way. A gift of freedom this soul had given me.

I could not wait to hold this life that had spent all this time growing in my belly. A life that was mine to love and give to. This soul had already given me so much, just being with me for the duration of these last months. I couldn't wait to give my all to this child. I was so very excited to grow into motherhood and understand what this really meant.

After the birth of my newborn baby, I went back to school. This was a time that I called a gathering of knowledge. I gathered knowledge while I had an only child and the opportunity to. I had enrolled in a community services course, but was declined as I needed a Year 11 completion certificate. I had previously not completed my high school education. This is where my adult education began: taking a local adult Year 11 class.

Being a country town with many remote students, the education institution allowed the 12 months of classes to take place at a local house. They also allowed me to take my baby to classes and take care of my baby's needs all throughout the days.

This house was only a 5 km walk from my house.

A couple of days a week, I would have to get up super early, before the sun even came up, to get us both ready to do the exhilarating walk. This

DYSFUNCTIONAL DEPENDANCIES

took me around 2 hours with my large pram and the hugest nappy bag you've ever seen to cart enough towelling nappies, changes of clothes, toys, and food for both of us. I turned up a few times drenched from the rain with hail-burnt fingertips. The pram was fitted with bulky wind and rain protectors. When others discovered I was walking, they kindly offered me lifts but none of the adult students had baby capsules or up to 12 month-approved car seats fitted in their vehicles. Anyway, I was happy to walk. Four hours of brisk walking and pushing a full pram which felt like a truck by the end of the day worked wonders on my weight loss and fitness regime. I had my post-baby bod back in less than 12 months with arms and legs that had the definition of an elite athlete!

I completed my Year 11. To be able to gain the further community services qualification I wanted, we needed to move to the town that had an instituition with the course available and a day care centre close by, as this larger institution did not allow children or have a day care facility.

We currently lived out of town and this town was over a 30-minute drive with no public transport. I enrolled into the new education institution not knowing how I was going to get there or how this was all going to come together, but I had faith that it would work out.

First and foremost, I began looking for a house to rent in town. I found one near the local shops, a family day care, and my partner's new place of employment.

This was still a two hour walk by the time I dropped my child at family day care and walked to the institution. I did this three days a week for the next 18 months. This did not bother me at all, except in the dreaded Victorian winter when storms and hail burnt my fingertips – umbrellas just didn't quite cover everything!

I became fitter than I had ever been and was super excited to learn what I could in order to begin my goal of working in the community sector, supporting people that had been through trauma, addictions, and/or lived with disabilities. Studying opened up a whole world I had no idea about. My love for learning grew and led to further education as time went on. This is where I discovered my love of writing. I began journaling my experiences and writing poetry.

My time when I wasn't studying was spent playing and teaching my child new things. I loved being a mum for so many reasons. Watching my child grow and learn had brought out my own inner child. I was planning on another baby once I had completed this qualification and work placement requirements.

I began volunteering two days a week in the community sector. One day was spent working for the Victorian Blind Association, supporting the vision impaired on community outings, skills development activities, making baskets, and building small furnishings. The other day was spent working at a community playhouse/day care and afterschool care for children from six months of age to primary school age. I could take my own child with me to the playhouse. A day we both looked forward to each week. The playhouse offered fun activities we both enjoyed and a great way to actively network with other mums and bubs, we were always meeting new people.

At this point, I took my now two-year-old son to visit my family and the place I once called home. The photo was taken in front of the shed I used to live in on my father's Harley Davidson.

DYSFUNCTIONAL DEPENDANCIES

As time went on, I continued working part-time and completed my studies. My second child was growing in my belly: my family was about to expand (and so was I)! After all the hard work getting my post-baby bod back, it was all about to go to AWOL.

I now proudly held two certificates. I got my drivers' license and bought my first car. I drove everywhere and began yet another course: an introduction to Reiki, alternate healing techniques, meditation, and self-awareness. This course was run by an amazing spiritual mentor. Synchronicity played a big role between us. As the years went on and I moved about interstate, we found each other every time I was ready for another alternative course in healing the soul. I walked into a few meditation circles and there she would be, magically waiting for me to take the next step toward my spiritual growth.

FACE *of* FAITH

After the exciting and miraculous birth of my second child, I could not wait to get home and share this new life with my family. I was hoping this new change would bring happiness to us all.

My home life was not as exciting. My homecoming shattered me with a painful reality. There was never a dull moment and some frightening ones too.

I waited all day for my lift home from the hospital, running down to the foyer and back upstairs to my new baby. The hospital rang home many times to no answer. I knew something wasn't right. We had no mobile phones back then, only landlines, and if they didn't get answered, there was no other form of contact. I had the hospital call home repeatedly until the end of the day. They insisted on calling me a taxi and someone who could go to my home to organise my baby capsule seat to take my new baby home to our family.

We were dropped off home. I walked through the back door with our newborn child in a capsule to a sight and smell that will never leave me! I saw a group of people around my kitchen table and my lounges in a house that I called my "family" home, with tightly bound tourniquets wrapped around their arms, needles still protruding from arms and hands, bent silver spoons, broken and smashed bottles of alcohol, bowls of drugs: an incoherent bunch of adults and the father of my now two children. I was speechless and so were they. Not one of them could put two words together! I looked around to find my child, my three-year-old playing quietly in his room with his door closed. I broke down and cried sitting on the bedroom floor with my two babies. This was jeopardising the safety and wellbeing of my children.

What was I to do? I was loving life outside my home, but inside, life was in turmoil. Drugs were still rampant in my home!

DYSFUNCTIONAL DEPENDANCIES

I realised at this point that nothing would change if I didn't do something. My partner was suffering from a very serious drug addiction. He was also the father of my two children. I had experienced firsthand the wrath and evil side of this addiction. I understood how difficult it was to overcome. Nevertheless, there was no excuse for this behaviour in front of my three-year-old. I made a decision that day that I was not going to allow this behaviour to take place in or near my family home or my children again.

That decision brought days and nights at home alone with the children, waiting for him to walk in the door, not knowing when their father was going to come home. Even when he was home, there became raging, angry outbursts of blame, shame, and pain. It was becoming an unhealthy environment for us all. My relationship became co-dependant, a spiralling whirlwind of his addictions while keeping it all hidden from the outside world. The role of victim and empath began to play out, over and over again. At the time, I just couldn't see it for what it was as I was caught up in my own "circle of dependency." The children were dependant on me, I was dependant on him, and he was dependant on his addictions.

Nevertheless, he loved his children. He did work hard at many jobs to provide for his family as best he could. All I wanted was to keep trying to fix the problem. I felt responsible for him and making things right for our family, which took away his own responsibility to help and heal himself as I had been doing with myself! The change I had worked towards and hoped for never came to fruition.

Whilst I had overcome my past and had been working hard, in every way rebuilding my own life, there was the devastating wrath of addiction playing out behind the scenes. I was lucky enough to see my way clear of it. He was not so lucky. Not from a lack of trying.

There were courageous attempts at rehabilitation. It was more a case of a lack of network, community support, and a lack of resilience. His struggle to recover was eating away at both of us.

At this point I was back working in the community in the disability sector, doing care work for the elderly and people with disabilities. I was still breastfeeding and expressing for the times I was away with clients. I was also beating myself up about my homelife, protecting my children, not being able to fix the world's problems or my own: what was I to do from here? Feeling helpless and confused, I dove into weekly therapy sessions and enrolled in yet another course – on counselling this time!

This inspired me to come up with a plan. Before I knew it, I was setting goals and smashing them one after the other.

I had discovered all I could change about my situation was my attitude towards it and the thought patterns that kept me stuck there. No more procrastinating! I decided I had learnt enough about myself and the devastating effects of addiction on my growing family! It was time we all move forward and grow from this.

I planned for a new beginning.

I literally opened an atlas off my bookshelf and picked a place to move to. Change would be as awesome as a holiday. I took the children for a holiday to the chosen place off the map and found a house to rent! We went home, packed up a trailer full of bedding and clothes and away we went to live a new life on a very pretty coastline of Australia.

DYSFUNCTIONAL DEPENDANCIES

Soon after, the children's father followed, after a lengthy rehabilitation. My dreams of a healthy and happy family were coming to fruition.

I was now strength training at a local gym, studying music and carrying my third child.

I was overwhelmed with feelings of love and this time around had experienced no morning sickness. I felt healthier and more energised than I had ever felt. My health and fitness regime was working that's for sure: I was jogging along with the pram these days. I went through another three brand-new prams over the next two years. Even the wheels couldn't keep up with me!

A few pregnancy and birth complications later, I brought a beautiful baby girl into the world. With her came waves of emotion due to the fact that I never had a mother-daughter relationship. I felt overwhelmed when I thought about how I was going to mother such a beautiful little girl. As the weeks and months passed, the love I felt just happened. We nurtured each other, we grew together, and all my fears fell away.

We finally bought a house of our very own. A huge double storey house: it even had a white picket fence! I grew vegetables and planted lots of pretty flowers, and created garden beds of them everywhere.

Meanwhile, all seemed ok on the surface, but I had seen the signs and knew them too well. My partner was sinking deeper into a depressive state. He was struggling with our expanding family, all the changes that were happening, and his mental health. He had spiralled again, becoming so physically and mentally unwell.

The substance abuse was kept hidden, out of sight, but not out of mind. The wrath of addictive and aggressive behaviours had escalated once again. There were many nights we waited for him to walk through the door, sometimes even days and nights on end. I waited for a phone call… not knowing whether it was going to be to pick him up from wherever he had ended up on these drug-induced occasions, or the police to notify us of the worst. Getting a phone call was always a sense of relief, even if it meant us driving to the local hospital or the police station to bring him home.

I realised at that point I was helpless to save him from his addictions. This was something only he could heal from, when he was ready.

It had become dysfunctional. Once again, the only thing I could change was the way I needed to deal with the situation. I was only responsible for myself and these wonderful children I had bought into the world. My priority was to protect myself and my family!

We needed to move forward from this and we did. We had agreed to separate and I helped him move into his own place.

I went back to work and began studying and gaining certifications in alternate healing therapies with the wonderful local spiritual mentor I had met years prior running her course in another state. I had been moving in a positive direction among inspiring meditation groups and circles. I was now juggling a toddler, day care, my work hours,

DYSFUNCTIONAL DEPENDANCIES

strength training, school activities, my children's sporting activities, and their regular visitation with their father, which was a bit of a distance to travel once he had moved interstate. I always made an effort for them to maintain a relationship with him.

I still found myself journaling in my spare time. I began writing lyrics to songs that I could sing while making up tunes on my guitar, and I became passionate about singing.

Eventually, I entered into a new relationship. There were many children involved. My family expanded into what seemed like the Brady Bunch. The house needed extensions: even though it was a double storey four bedroom, the extra bedroom and bathroom were welcomed, as was the new supersized pot and pan set to cook for our football-team sized family!

I decided I needed a long holiday: so much had happened and some time to process and enjoy living was what my heart yearned for at this point. I put the house on the market and began an adventure, travelling Australia for 18 months in a large motorhome with my extra-large family.

Shortly after the trip began, the phone call came, the one I had anxiously waited for… the passing of my children's father.

I felt deeply saddened with grief, for our children, the last time they would speak to him was days before over the phone. With my grief, there was also a sense of relief that his struggle was over, he could now be at peace.

Near the end of this book is a self-help journal with a goal-setting guide. If you have an addiction, or know someone close to you who does, seek support, call for an intervention, or call for help. There are many avenues for support these days! Don't wait! You're only waiting for death. Just do it – call someone! Make this a part of your own self-help journal.

I can tell you there is life on the other side of addiction and it is *never* too late! I am backing you 100% to seek support for you, your family member, or your friend. But you must also back yourself in taking those steps forwards in your own recovery.

CHAPTER 4

WHISPERS OF LOVE

A caring woman prepares her young

A warm soulful day for everyone

As the stars sparkle late at night

The moon shines through its healing light

The trees speak in their rustling leaves

Sharing words of love and feelings of ease.

WHISPERS OF LOVE

Whilst my children and I were grieving the loss of their father, we shared many moments of tears and fears, anger and hugs, solitude, and even gratitude that we all still had each other.

As difficult as it was some days, I continued to support them, to put one foot in front of the other, and soldier on. I had learnt life had its ups and its downs, we would ride it out together, no matter what!

We were developing a property I had bought in Queensland. We spent some time parked on this property whilst building a double garage and fitting out another 40-foot coach, which was slightly bigger than the one we were living in at the time. This one turned into a luxurious set up: fully-equipped with 12 volt lighting, a 10 kVA generator, and solar power to run everything from a television and X-Box to laptops to the laundry we had built in to the under floor bins, a split system air-conditioner/heater, and spa! This was luxury, with all the bells, whistles, and comfort we needed to travel around in.

After the completion of the property investment development, we journeyed on to explore more of the Australian countryside.

I was home-schooling and incorporating excursions into the Steiner education learning modules. Engaging closely with my children and step-children was a beautiful gift. We all became close living in each other's pockets. Not only did we eat together and watch movies together, like we had done before travelling, we went everywhere together and slept in beds only a metre apart, talking each other to sleep some nights!

The early mornings included a "morning ritual" of sitting around in a circle at the altar I created at the front of the coach. This was a beautiful gratitude gathering the children and I had been doing regularly, even before we left our home for our travelling adventures.

At the altar was displayed a large picture of the goddess Isis, the protector of women and children, a collection of candles, and incense to burn, which created a beautiful sight and scent for all our senses to smile! There was also a big bowl of regularly cleansed crystals we often used during our gratitude meditation.

We would spend around 30 minutes listening to a relaxation, meditating, chanting mantras or Tibetan healing sounds with our own voices in and out of harmony. After we set our intent for the day and centred ourselves, we would take it in turns to pick one thing or person within our lives, and say something we appreciated about them. This was an amazing way to begin our day and brought a feeling of gratitude and love into our lives.

Afterward, we would do a daily exercise routine to activate the brain, something vigorous like a 20-minute cardio workout, a ball game, or a run. We all enjoyed this routine, most of the time. There were some "I'm grumpy, I can't be bothered, I have nothing nice to say about anything" attitudes some days, and even I had my moments...! After all, there were seven of us all living under each other's feet and some of us were still grieving.

It wasn't always as rosy as I had planned it to be. The main thing is the intention was always a positive one that came from a kind heart space.

WHISPERS OF LOVE

The days and nights were so busy at times that we were all exhausted by the end of it, travelling from place to place with "white line fever," always eager to get to and explore the next destination. We took many school excursions around the countryside to places that our Australian explorers discovered and put on the map, as well as places of pure red dirt, where we bathed in fresh hot water springs and hot bore water that would pour out of holes on the walls in public bathroom blocks.

There were so many of us on board, all at different ages and stages of life and learning. Each day was structured around day-to-day activities and scheduled schooling, from breakfast, second breakfast, lunch, second lunch, dinner, second dinner – there was *always* seconds, insisted on by the children and never a scrap left on a plate! Being busy and active every day sure made us a hungry bunch.

I had many late nights preparing the following day's schooling program, excursions, activities, and healthy homemade meals. When I say healthy, I mean *healthy*. We ate as organic and fresh as possible, from individually chosen organic ingredients that made our own homemade muesli and daily baked bread to an assortment of vegetarian bakes and dishes. At times, cooking was a part of our schooling sessions, learning about food, health, food hygiene, meal preparation, and putting together ingredients for international round-the-world dishes. We sure made some gourmet and delicious meals. The children and I could have started a "My Coach Kitchen Rules" business with the dishes we made, some of which were totally our own creation!

In our new coach, we had an approved all-white leather and tiled tattoo studio set up so we could earn money on the road designing artworks for clients and tattooing from town to town. We were also working out of tattoo parlours as my partner at the time was a tattoo artist.

In my spare time, I wrote song lyrics, and sang all kinds of music. I met a few singer-songwriters along the way and was able to practise getting up on stage and singing a song or two with them. I was blessed during my travels to meet and chat with some of the greatest musicians of all time.

I needed to cancel a few bookings I had made across Australia as I was stuck in an outback town for two months or so, waiting on mechanical parts for the front part of the coach to be repaired after an incident with a giant outback kangaroo – bigger than any human I have ever seen. The kangaroos and wildlife looked like they were all on steroids out the outback of Australia!

Locals had mentioned certain roads were blocked off during wet weather seasons. Due to this, a journey in a different direction was planned. I had served breakfast and, of course, second breakfast. We did the morning routine meditation, chants, and mantras, sitting in our circle of gratitude. Then we journeyed on, leaving the outback town to head on the long journey to inland NSW to a well-known country music festival with my song lyrics and the $25,000 worth of music gear I had purchased to meet up with other musicians and begin my career performing as a singer-songwriter! I felt super excited to be on this journey. Off we went, with an altered travel plan and white line fever setting in. There was a long distance to travel over the next five days.

Little did I realise at this point that the Universe had something else in store, something other than what I had planned and had been working towards. It seemed like a normal happy day, but would be the last day of our travelling adventures.

We came across some small towns, one with Japanese gardens and a hot spa spring and stopped for a swim. We always welcomed a swim as the heat was unbearable at times. After enjoying lunch at the gardens and collecting some really cool bits for the children's travel boxes that they had been filling with collections of an assortment of things on our travels, we journeyed on.

There became an issue with the towbar on the coach. It had come loose from towing a car trailer with a second-hand vehicle on it that we just purchased days prior. The vehicle was backed off the trailer and I drove the vehicle behind the coach until the next caravan park where we could pull up and have it repaired.

My stepson had wanted to travel with me to keep me company in the car. We were singing along to some of our favourite tunes and driving along at the 100 km speed limit.

Not long after we hopped in that car, the life we had was about to change dramatically!

Suddenly, the steering of this vehicle became tight, crabbing and jamming. I tried with all my strength to pull the steering wheel around back onto the road so we didn't roll down into the big square outback drains – this was where we were headed if I didn't do something fast! Within seconds, the steering wheel was completely locked and we were headed into a gully towards trees. The last thing I remember was braking and taking a hand off the steering wheel, grabbing my young stepson by his shirt and seatbelt to hold him still whilst he was screaming in fear.

FACE of FAITH

In those moments, I said out loud a deep prayer for our survival. This was a tragic moment we shared and a day neither of us will ever forget.

CHAPTER 5

SOUL SCARS

Her eyes flickered what seemed their last moments of fate,

Her heart fell into an unconscious state,

Tears wept inside her broken body and soul,

As she was swept away from her human role,

Time passes, held in suspension,

As she experiences another dimension,

Whispers of love came rushing through,

An angel saved her life, as this whirlwind blew.

SOUL SCARS

A perfect, sunny day in November 2004: the day that tore my world apart. A terrible accident that turned my life upside down and inside out, a significant change in the direction I was heading!

It all happened so suddenly. I was totally alert: I hadn't had any alcohol or fallen asleep. There was no negligence on my part. It was all due to a mechanical failure in the steering of the vehicle that my partner at the time had purchased on a trip 12 days prior. The steering jammed, causing me to lose control and hit a large tree.

My face smashed directly into the timber steering wheel that was fitted to the vehicle. I discovered it had no airbags or seat belt retraction and that timber steering wheels are much tougher than my skull!

I missed moments of time as the carnage unfolded. I lost consciousness and, with that, my memory of what happened. The last thing I remembered to my first recollections of consciousness was never regained.

While I hung, physically dying through clogged airways and blood loss, trapped in the front seat with the front half of the vehicle caved in around us, my brave ten-year-old stepson, with all his fear and courage and his own injury, climbed from the wreckage through the broken glass window and ran for help. He ran until he found men working on a railway line nearby. He rushed them back to where I sat, heavy and unconscious, bleeding almost to my death.

The outside of my face was completely ripped apart and two-thirds of the bone structure of my face and frontal skull was protruding, crushed, and bleeding. I can only imagine how frightening this must have looked to a 10-year-old child. Regardless, he saved my life! He was my angel that day.

The next thing I remembered was hearing his very brave tears and soft, quivering voice trying to talk to me, telling me he had run and found people to help me. He was sitting beside me trying to comfort my broken body. These men who had been working on the railway that day were repeatedly telling me that help was on its way and that I had had an accident. They had carried me unconscious out of the vehicle, holding me upright against a tree, using what materials they had on them to help control the bleeding.

I was delirious, coming in and out of consciousness. I remember only small pieces. I could hear many voices faintly fading in and out through the gruesome sound of my body trying to breathe through my throat, almost drowning in my own outpouring of blood. A sound I will never forget! I put my hand up to what was once my face and felt wet, crushed bones flattened and bits protruding in areas they weren't supposed to be. I couldn't see anything, there was just blackness. I wasn't able to speak very well and what noises I was making were not anything I could even figure out. I really wasn't sure what was happening or what had happened, but I felt no pain at all, only waves of nausea between waking moments of consciousness.

I heard a few words fading in and out from the paramedics talking amongst themselves. They were saying that a helicopter was on its way but she won't make it to the hospital, we are not able to control the blood loss and internal bleeding, she is not breathing well and her blood pressure is dropping quickly. Another paramedic suggested giving me as much morphine as they could to make me comfortable in the meantime. As I heard those words, I wanted to tell them I was

SOUL SCARS

ok. I was alive and I could hear them. I wanted to tell them I was not going to die, but my mind and body were fighting to stay alive!

I felt someone holding my hand and a lady's voice trying to talk to me. She was asking me questions about my life and family to bring me around, keep me awake. I tried to answer her questions, but speaking and trying to communicate was almost impossible. Sometime later, I heard the helicopter arrive.

As I was being lifted into the helicopter I had my first recollection of hearing my family's voices, all crying in the distance. They had been travelling up the road in the coach in front of us, totally unaware that the accident had happened until emergency services were able to make contact with them after the incident

I was airlifted to a coastal hospital, hours away from this outback town in a gully full of trees where the accident had happened. I have vague memories of the flight. Each time I came into consciousness, I would violently vomit. I could hear and feel the paramedics talking to me nervously in loud voices, holding my hands and rubbing my legs, telling me to stay with them. I could hear them using medical apparatuses available to them. My body was fighting for its life and so were they. I felt tired and couldn't keep myself awake. I was dying.

My arrival and time at that hospital for the weeks before my transfer to another hospital was a blur of emergency surgery, living in a shadow of darkness, unable to see anything but contrasts of dark and light, sickness, and being cared for from head to toe, in every way.

I survived!

The day I was being transferred to another hospital, the medical professionals advised me I would not be able to travel by air for the distance required due to the damage and pressure built up in my skull. The crushed bones were beginning to set in their places, and needed to be reconstructed immediately if the bone structure was to ever have any sort of recognisable facial structure again. The hospital where I needed further emergency surgery was 15 hours from the hospital I was in. They had no transportation to travel this far except by air, which was not agreeable to the damage to my skull. It was agreed I would be heavily sedated and transferred with my family. This was to be the first time the children and I had seen each other since the accident. They were terribly upset and crying as I was wheeled to our coach, strapped down to the lounge, and given super strong medication to keep me sleeping most of the way. Due to "no coach parking" or caravan park coach parking at the major city hospital I was headed to, it had been arranged to take the children and the coach to a friend's house on the way for the duration of my hospital stay. These friends had a long and steep uphill driveway in the mountain hinterlands of the Sunshine Coast. The rain was heavy and the steep, uphill driveway was boggy. The back end of the 40-foot coach and the empty trailer on the back slid off the edge of the steep gully beside the driveway. The owners of the property drove the tractor down and hooked up chains to the coach to tow it up. As the tractor began sliding with the coach, this was not successful. It slid down until it found a resting place against a huge tree. The coach was on so much of a downwards angle, the door was wedged into the ground and jammed shut! It took some time for others to bend the door and wedge it open enough to hand the children through one at a time. I could hear the fear in everyone's voices! Then I was passed through the area that was wedged open. It was difficult to see as I could still only make out silhouettes on lighter contrasts. We made our way up to their house.

SOUL SCARS

These friends lent us a vehicle to get me to the hospital. This day was a long and exhausting trip for all. The pain that seemed a nine out of ten, ten being the worst ever, had over the last few hours become unbearable. If I had to rate it on a scale of one thousand, it would have been two thousand! Tears were flowing down my face for the rest of the way.

I arrived at this hospital around 2 am without my transfer documentation of what had happened and what I was booked in to have done, as this folder was left in the coach that was still resting against a large tree halfway down a gully!

As I tried to explain why I was there and crying in pain, they gave me a bed in Emergency but were not able to give me anything for pain until a doctor had completed assessments and made contact with the previous hospital.

From here, physical pain became a very familiar part of my life and this hospital became my second home for the next ten years.

My vision was still poor: silhouettes and shadows were all I could make out. My face felt a mangled mess, with bones crushed and setting in places they were not meant to be.

As this week went on, before the first reconstruction, my vision improved slightly as the swelling and pressure subsided. As part of my rehabilitation, I was put in front of a mirror. I went into shock, my heart raced, and I collapsed to the ground, unconscious! My face was unrecognisable – there wasn't one. It was mangled, my lips torn in half, the bone structure flattened in multiple places, no nose at all with black and blue bruising. When I woke up I was back in my hospital bed. I couldn't believe it: I was never going to have the face I had ever again. It was gone. All this talk of reconstruction was going to need to create a whole new facial structure!

This accident had not only impacted my life, but the lives of my family. My children had just been exposed to a very traumatic experience that was out of my control. Their innocent fun-filled childhood of travelling, adventures and our lives how I planned it, had come to a tragic end. My family were soon to become my carers as, for a long time, I could not care for myself.

That day tore not only my world apart, it stripped away the face I always knew when I looked in the mirror: the face my family and friends knew as Shelley! My children were afraid of how I looked and of losing me as I struggled through that first year of rehabilitation. My four-year-old daughter would not come near me for that whole entire year. I had to find ways I could communicate with her. I would place scarves or put a pillow up to hold over my face to talk to her. Our conversations would lead to her saying, "You sound like my Mummy but I don't know where she went!" She would ask me where her mummy went, over and over! She changed her name and mine to deal with the loss of my identity and the mother she knew.

This was shattering! My role as a mother had taken a backseat, and so had my role as a teacher. It was like a death, a loss of who I was, what I looked like, the personality I had, the life I lived: the me that I was, was gone! It was a miracle I had survived, but with that miracle of my life came a death. I had emotionally and mentally died. I couldn't think clearly or speak properly without stuttering terribly, my brain was failing me. What was happening to me? The rebirth from this life experience was to take a long time.

SOUL SCARS

My ten-year journey of head surgeries and medical interventions was underway. A great team of specialists began the process of rebuilding my internal facial bone structure and treating complications under the instruction and guidance of one of the best surgeons in the country – in the world, in fact! I began to see I was blessed and grateful to have his hands involved in every aspect of my surgical interventions. When he first approached me, saying what they needed to do in medical terms, I asked what he meant. He said, "Well, we have to cut the skin on your head from side to side, one ear to the other and peel the flap down off the frontal skull and face to rebuild. When we are finished, we staple you back together…" I was to go through this procedure and shave my hair off almost every year for the next six years.

I made countless and what seemed like endless trips to hospital. It was my second home – even the faces became familiar. With each and every trip to hospital whether by train, bus, car or Saint John ambulance, all I could think about was my children: whether my role as a mother would ever be like it was again and how I could help them through their suffering due to these lengthy, ongoing medical interventions.

Hospital and medical reports were being created from some amazing specialists on my team, including maxillo-facial, infectious bone disease, neurologists, [ENT] ear nose and throat, physiotherapists, occupational therapists, neuropsychologists, and pain management specialists performing tests scans, operations, administering treatment and more treatment. These reports stated all kinds of complications and permanent diagnoses that would impact the rest of my life: a crushed frontal skull wall, acquired brain injury, an infectious bone disease (pseudomonas) and staph, two bone infections. One bone infection was treatable, and one was not so treatable: it was incurable, in fact. This developed and grew inside my skull, hiding in the titanium metal plates and eating away at bone until the bone matter died. This eventually made me very sick, and I was given less than two years to live!

Then there was my obliterated frontal sinuses, chronic migraines, multiple disorders in the DSM-IV related to brain injury and trauma. I was written off as never being capable of working in the workforce or having any kind of job in the community again.

Whilst enduring all of this, along came another diagnosis that was unrelated but not entirely. Due to all the anxiety, stress, fear, and the chemicals our brain produces whilst under these kinds of stresses, my body had developed cervical cancer! I had been undergoing medical treatment and minor surgical procedures to prevent this prior to the diagnosis.

As the years went on, I was using everything I physically had to fight this disease and illness but mentally I was scared and scattered. I was now concerned with two major out-of-control diseases thriving in my body. For the first time, I felt I was doomed. That was it: I didn't think I could physically take any more. I knew my body was resilient, *but not that resilient!*

At that point, I realised I was losing hope and faith in myself and all this fear I felt was not helping me heal.

Chronic illness and pain continued before, during, and after the reconstructive operations. I didn't know how I was going to survive, if I could at all.

SOUL SCARS

I began consulting alternative healing therapies and using some of the great healing tools that I had learnt through my life. Then I discovered yoga.

I began to stick positive and loving affirmations all around the house and only whisper the word "pseudomonas" when needed in order to avoid giving this disease any more power over me, hoping my cells would not hear it anymore!

It was frightening knowing this bone disease was growing inside my skull and there was nothing medically that could be done to stop it. When I asked my surgeon how to get rid of it and what had been done before, he said, "We can try the treatment process and any other ideas you have to throw the book at it. Because if it were an arm or leg, they would amputate…" I guess decapitation wasn't really allowed in this day and age!

I began educating myself on all aspects of what was happening to me physically, emotionally, and medically while the three monthly lots of treatment began to contain this infectious disease, helping only to slow down the spread, due to its resistance to treatment and ability to hide inside metal plates. It was really an ongoing treatment process.

I went to visit a Traditional Chinese Medicine practitioner/naturopath with an extended reputation for healing any illness. I began taking prescribed remedies he made to assist my body to fight this.

I consulted with the Chinese medicine practitioner weekly over 12 months. He taught me that our bodies are easy to heal, but the mind plays an even bigger part in our recovery. Working on the mind is just as important.

Not only did I have a physical battle I was fighting, I had lost my face, the face that was familiar when I looked in the mirror. It was my identity and who I felt I was as a woman. I needed to unpack all that for the healing of my body, mind, and soul to take place.

As I delved into this inner journey, it was also important for me to follow medical advice from my team with the next steps to take.

My body was tired. I was fighting with EVERYTHING and maintaining a very organic, healthy vegetarian diet. Everything was homemade, with no processed foods or alcohol at all. I had multiple natural and pharmaceutical medicinal treatment to treat all medical problems.

I was practising yoga more regularly now, learning to breathe deeply while exercising my mind, body, and soul. Slowing down my mind showed me all the parts of myself that were out of balance and in need of healing. There was a lot that needed healing! My body was in knots, and everything felt wrong inside and out. My entire skull was screaming in pain internally, I couldn't even hear myself think. My thoughts were clouded and overwhelming a lot of the time. I struggled even speaking most days.

I had two surgeries that were both kind of urgent. I contacted my surgeon and asked which should I have first: the next head operation to scrape the bone infection out or to remove the early detection of cervical cancer?

SOUL SCARS

"Definitely have the cancer removed first," was my surgeon's reply.

The surgery was a success as I had hoped. This was lucky for me, as two days later we were moving back to Queensland to a farm that I had found online. Now, I could continue intense treatment, further surgery, and lengthy hospital stays with only eight hours travel to the hospital. This was much closer than the two return flights it was taking me from where I was living! This was a busy few days of unpacking and enrolling all the children into their new schools.

I bought the first one-year-old yearling horse I had had in a long time, and the first horse my children had experienced. This was to be one of many horses I owned as I began rescuing horses in need of help, physically or psychologically. I was in much need of horse therapy.

It had been one week since the removal of the cervical cancer and I haemorrhaged badly. I was rushed to the nearest hospital, then rushed by ambulance to another hospital. My memory had faded as to what happened upon arriving at the second hospital. Convulsions began and I was losing consciousness. I was given blood transfusions for the next eight hours.

My body had almost given up and I nearly died *again*. I was mentally and physically exhausted, but alive! I was starting to realise that although I was struggling to function on so many levels, there was some greater purpose for my existence because, against all odds, I was still in the land of the living.

I actually woke up laughing as I had envisioned a dream of a woman standing beside me all night with a tube running from her arm into mine. She was telling me this would give me new life and help heal my broken body so I could go on to do the things that I was meant to do in this life.

What was I meant to be doing? I had many questions now. I could not remember all of what she had communicated, but it was as though she was talking to me the entire night. I felt my spirit beginning to stir from a long sleep. There was work to be done, but first I had to work on myself and get well. Given the physical, mental, environmental, and emotional state I was in, I knew this was not going to happen overnight!

I was very sick, physically spent in every way. It was getting harder to get out of bed, but life required it. I never knew it was possible for my body to sleep upright until now, with one arm on the toilet seat, my head resting against my arm and my back against the wall as exhaustion set in. There was no energy left inside me I did not care where my head rested. It all became totally irrelevant! This sickness came and went.

This was to be the rock bottom point of this illness and the horrendous and chronic pain I was enduring. It felt worse than at the bottom of a rock let me tell you. This had been going on for years. I felt so weak. My weight plummeted to its lowest: 48 kg. I looked sick, and I didn't know how I would have the physical strength for another major surgery and recovery. I really had nothing left to fight with!

At this point, my illness and struggle to get well had taken a huge toll on my marriage. Everything began to fall apart, with my focus on surviving and his engagements drawing him closer to the unruly world of club life that I kept my distance from. My father had moved in with us for a while to help take care of my family.

SOUL SCARS

Before the operation, I had a huge adult tantrum in front of my father, saying that it wasn't fair, I just couldn't keep going on. I was refusing to go through with it because I didn't think I would survive and my family had suffered for long enough. I would just live my days out from here. My father had said, "Life is not fair, but regardless, the choice is yours to make and everything happens for a reason. Look at all that's happened. You survived it all, you are strong and you will get through it, but only you can decide what you do from here."

I gave myself time to prepare. At that time, I decided I had nothing to lose and was preparing my body and began gaining a little weight. I owed this to my children.

My more recent and eight weekly scans had also showed a positive result: this infectious disease in my skull was shrinking. My surgeon had told me that the blood transfusions I had previously had were a blessing in disguise. The fresh blood had assisted my body to produce new blood cells, promoting bone marrow growth, assisting in bone healing: another miracle. While we're revealing miracles, a very tiny deviation had tunnelled from my obliterated sinuses, creating a small passage for drainage. Healing was taking place!

I had moved to another state onto a farm with all my horses for work purposes, opened another tattoo studio, and had another major surgery a year or so later. The first few photos are before the final surgery and others are after this final surgery.

FACE of FAITH

SOUL SCARS

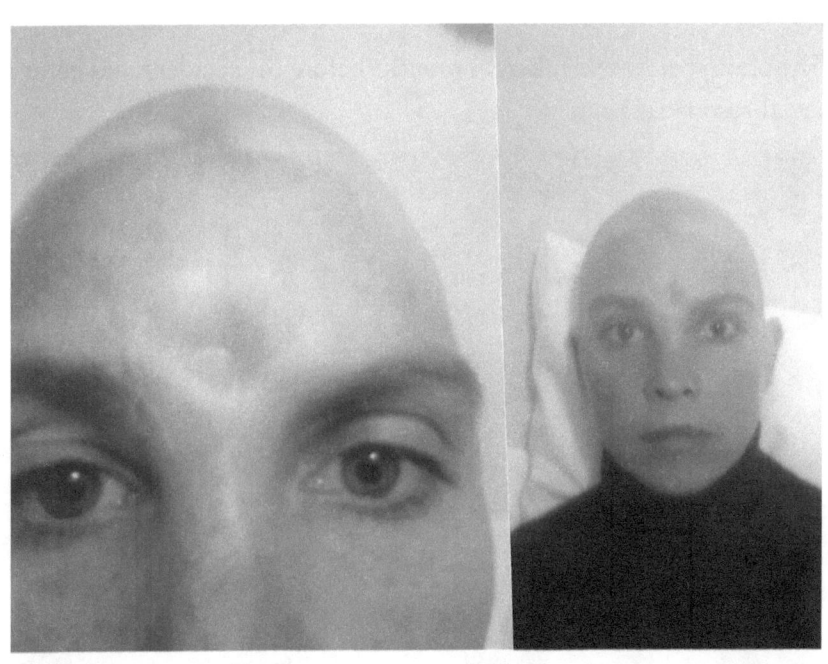

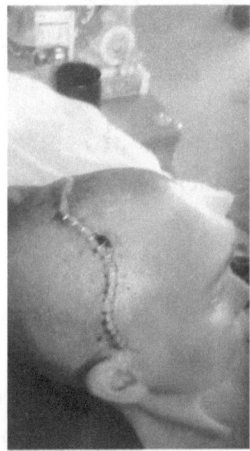
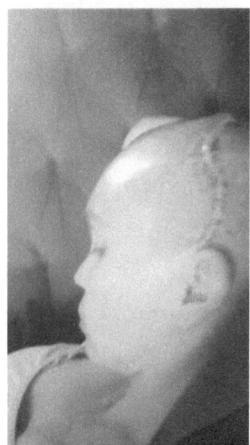

The photo below was taken 18 months before the accident and before facial reconstruction.

It had been over six years since the first emergency surgery after being airlifted the day of the accident.

With each major operation came a long 12-month recovery. My environment remained chaotic and always busy, with a supersized family of children coming and going, organising the children's week to week activities, and the moving around we had done to open our own tattoo studios. Managing tattoo shops was political and chaotic. In my time, art was only half of the tattoo industry, the other half was a war waiting to happen! So, my stress levels were high. I couldn't change what was happening around me, so I continued practising mindful breathing to slow it all down. All I could do was slow myself down internally and let the healing happen.

SOUL SCARS

My relationship had endured sufferings of an unrestrained and harsh lifestyle of hardships and betrayal and had inevitably come to an end. He left and I filed for divorce, knowing this wouldn't be easy and would have its repercussions, but it was a step forward in the changes I needed to make.

This whole entire experience from that day in November 2004 was destined to bring me great changes: the change I needed to become the face of faith. These scars that were destined to be, through hope, adversity, miracles, resilience, and rehabilitation was born this face of faith. I kept journaling, hoping I could put it all together into a book one day.

CHAPTER 6

UNRESTRAINED ANARCHY

I knew too much hate to feel that love was real,

I witnessed too much evil to accept ascension exists,

I felt too much sadness to know the meaning of true happiness,

I felt an angry war in my heart to feel any peace on this earth,

I lived too much hardship to understand the meaning of the words ease and grace,

I experienced the vile greed of human nature, and was stripped of all I held dear,

FACE *of* FAITH

But somewhere within

I could feel ascension exists,

A peace growing in my heart,

True happiness is within

Sharing is a given and a part of life

And love is real and present in all things

Even the scars.

UNRESTRAINED ANARCHY

During the medical side of things, I went through a long legal battle for almost eight years awaiting a large payment of compensation. This legal battle came to an abrupt end when I received a phone call from my barrister and solicitor explaining my position in this twisted game they play and the lunch meeting they had with the insurance company. They had backed me into a corner and they ended the "no win no fee" policy after more than seven years. They suggested I start paying big money if I wanted to proceed to trial. This would be an upfront amount of $30,000 to be deposited that day and a further amount of around $60,000-$70,000 to be deposited into their account before the trial date (only weeks away), to allow for more evidence reports and lengthy trial costs incurred. My ongoing medical impairments were clearly evident and so was the mechanical failure of the vehicle. It had been heavily documented and reported by multiple mechanical engineers: many major components of the steering and front end had been previously worked on and failed the safety inspection multiple times, passing only days prior to the purchasing of the vehicle. The mechanical fault was described as evidence of what had happened! But third-party compensation claim laws are complex and different in the state of Queensland and the police never submitted a "complete report" of the vehicle or the incident!

My other option was, if I lost the trial due to what they were telling me was a "lack of evidence," I would lose what I put up as well as have to pay all other parties' years of legal and trial costs.

I wondered whose legal team they were actually on, because it didn't seem they were batting for mine!

Either way, this was going to cost me more energy than I had to give and a lot of money that I didn't have to spare, as I had sold all my assets to financially provide for my family during my time of bedbound illness. Not to mention, I had just been through an unruly divorce settlement!

More chapters had ended. It was a relief to sign off on all the dotted lines. I felt a sense of surrender, freeing myself of the things I no longer wanted in my life. I was not completely out of the woods and still in the early stages of yet another recovery, but with all these endings, this was an opening for new opportunities to focus on and financially I knew we would be ok. We are lucky in our country to have government income to support our families during times of need and lack of income!

Yet what followed was as I had expected. Inside of an unruly world without disciplined systems and of unrestrained anarchy, I had given in to the mind-blowing political propositions and the repercussions I knew were inevitable and not in my financial favour: I handed over what was demanded and filled up the pockets of sociopathic greed! With my false sense of freedom came a price my entire family paid physically, emotionally, and mentally! Unintentionally, I found myself still living within the constraints of this unlawful club lifestyle in a relationship with a man overseeing my every move: where for any of my kindness and loyalty given there was even more taken and all things taken for granted. I lived a life on the receiving end of emotional control, degrading abuse, betrayal, sexual exploitation, and dishonourable acts of violation so great it made it difficult to see my way forward through my recovery. Hell, it made it difficult to breathe and even though I was present, at times I felt absent.

Many frightening experiences at this time I will never forget, but just one I will share here to tell the bigger picture: getting dragged by my hair and thrown out of a car in the middle of the night onto the gutter in the pouring rain 6 km from my house because I refused to participate in activities that were not right for me! I became emotionally and mentally bruised. I was fractured with what I call a dysplasia of the mind. I realised at that point that I had been here before, in positions of vulnerability. I was well aware this was not healthy but I was unable to escape the confines and control of this situation at that time.

I learnt to step back, choosing only the battles that held importance. Self-preservation went a long way and was a way to protect myself from further harm.

My vision had become blurry, the fog was thickening again, becoming awfully hazy within my environment. My body still in the recovery process. I experienced nausea, loss of appetite, and weight loss.

Meanwhile, I had come to terms with living with a head injury and brain impairment, as frustrating as it was on some days when my motor functions were not how I would like them to be.

I was determined to rid myself completely of the infectious bone disease in my frontal skull. I had a strong will to get well, remaining focused on the recovery plan I had created for myself.

I began working through the mayhem, continuing on my journey, whilst I turned a blind eye to the many things going on behind the scenes. I was attending gym classes, strength training, cardio and yoga classes to heal from the inside out, strengthening every aspect of myself. I enrolled in a local education institution, doing extra modules in subjects I wanted to learn about, including drug and alcohol, mental health, and domestic violence – all the things that were familiar to me in my own experiences.

My passion for horses was a full-time job at home. Whilst studying, rescuing, training, and rehoming horses was rewarding, and a great experience for my growing family, it was also therapeutic in my recovery. I came across my second-biggest horse challenge when I was told about a wild, untamed, and unbroken mare who was born with brain damage and left in with cattle for ten years as no trainer could get near her. I got her in a float after weeks of visits. Then the fun began! She looked like the world's best bronco but would shake herself into a crippling mess and fall to the ground in total fear. Connecting and building trust with a psychologically destroyed, oversized animal was challenging, but I understood what it meant to have a fractured mind. I knew all too well, in fact, living in the realms of mind dysplasia! Without any force, just a lead rope, she began to wait at the gate for me. She became the sweetest horse to ride, loving human company so much she would come through the back door if it were left open. She became so pleasing and kind-hearted. ♥

My sense of will became stronger, but I felt a great sadness for all that I had not yet grieved. My role as a mother had changed dramatically over the years as my children became my full-time carers, taking great care of me on the days, weeks, and at times months, when I couldn't care for myself. They did for me what I was supposed to (and used to) do for them. I had lost my independence and become dependent on others when I was previously an extremely independent woman. I had lost my dreams and the woman I thought I was going to be. My face had changed with each surgery and it was not only the mirror reflecting these changes: the way others looked at me also changed. The impact this journey to wellness was having on my family was huge, as was the impact my own guilt and grief was having on my recovery. Many emotions swept over me. It was time to grieve! I finally allowed myself to cry, to grieve all the emotional aspects that needed to be released. I mean, I would break down and cry during a movie,

Photos of the beautiful stallion I had from a yearling.

a dance class, when a song would come on or when all my horses would break the fences, run away together, and all come galloping back the next day!

Whilst I was forever fixing broken fence lines to keep in my free-spirited stallion who would lead his herd away into the wilderness for a night here and there, I was oblivious to all things going on behind the scenes among the unruly and rebellious!

Another unpleasant experience happened within my family.

Around 4 am, while we lay in our beds sleeping, I heard the loudest bang. My front door had just been kicked in and 15 law enforcement officers came scrambling up my hallway. They kicked my bedroom door in, forcing their way in to all the bedrooms. I lay naked, frightened, and crying while three guns were pointed directly towards where I lay. We were held at gunpoint with loud voices demanding I stop crying. I was pleading with them not to go into my children's rooms or point guns at my children and begged to know what was going on. I was so frightened and could hear the fear in the voices of my children, enduring their own experience of it all. I tried to get out of bed, to go to my children, but was thrown back on the bed and told I would be handcuffed, tasered, and dragged outside if I moved again. My partner at the time was put in another room. Yes, it is like the movies portray it, only much worse and frightening to go through in real life! I was pulled aside and told to get dressed and get my children ready for school as normal under supervision of two of the force team, whilst the rest of them pulled the house and property apart for the next seven hours!

I had to find a way to turn this unruly life of fear I was living into freedom! I began making plans to relocate away from the situation we were in. It wasn't easy and took some months to pack my family's

UNRESTRAINED ANARCHY

things and find a place to rent which was affordable and closer to extended family. I was not sure of the hows and wheres of it all but preparing was essential. I sadly sold and gave away every one of our horses, even the ones I wanted to keep. That was one thing I had learnt: nothing is forever, life is ever changing! I spent the next few months working towards ticking off the "to do" list of everything that needed to be achieved to reach my main goal.

CHAPTER 7

FEAR TO FREEDOM

*The things that mattered before,
may not matter anymore,*

*Blinded by pain and fret,
wasted energy on anger and upset,*

*Change remains constant, what remains no longer
only makes us stronger,*

*A shift in focus, a shift in time, surrender is the key
to letting life be,*

*Rigid views left behind, movements in the process of
thought,
healing of the mind, body, and soul I sought.*

FEAR TO FREEDOM

Before the relocation, I had been attending a local Buddhist temple and received an initiation into Buddhism by a well-known lama who was travelling and teaching in our country that year. After my initiation and teachings I felt a sense of strength and freedom, learning to breathe fully into my body and practising becoming present and mindful in my day-to-day activities. It was taking some practise!

This group of people were my most influential supports in opening my mind to keep walking forward on my healing journey to freedom.

I had managed to make the huge move, crossing another border of this country, finally freeing myself, and my family, from an unruly lifestyle.

Sometime after the relocation and recuperation from all the hard work getting there, I had transferred my studies to another education institution, receiving recognition of prior learning for some core units. Further qualifications gave me the knowledge and ability to work within the community, doing what I love: supporting others within the disability and mental health sectors. I remained focused and tapped into all kinds of community and therapeutic activities, taking far better care of myself in more ways than I had been, learning to put myself before others – tough work for a giver!

What followed our new life was a cruel torment and mental manipulation that targeted my entire family. My breath was only half filling my lungs again, even during a yoga session.

I still found myself on the receiving end of all kinds of manipulating and threatening behaviours from the situation I had walked away from challenging my way forward.

But I proceeded to do whatever it took to keep my family safe! This manipulating behaviour was stamped on the minds and hearts of my family like an invisible scar, running deeper than the iceberg that sits underneath the waterline.

Living with that kind of fear caused damage that would take time, trust, and learning the art of *really* loving myself to heal all those unintegrated parts of myself that were wounded. As I had just gone from living a life of fear-based perception – always in a state of fear with the fight or flight response activated, waiting for what was going to happen next, ready to either run from the bear or fight the bear – to a totally different lifestyle!

A new place, a new space, a new hope, and a new life to create whatever we wanted and how we wanted it to be. My new face and this sense of freedom I now had was also very new, but it could not become a life of freedom without cleaning up the past and all the present and cruel repercussions that presented themselves. I made a paper trail over multiple community services of my story and what was happening as well as putting law-enforced measures in place to protect my family! I had empowered myself with a new sense of self-worth. It was *not* ok for others to bully, intimidate, manipulate, or threaten. It was my right to protect us from it all.

AAAAAHHHHH! Finally, I was breathing huge sighs of relief. With that flowed a river of tears. I no longer felt afraid; the fear was gone!

FEAR TO FREEDOM

I just didn't feel it anymore. I began to let go and breathe deeper as I found calm.

Breaking free of the controlled, hostile, and violent-fuelled environment, my tears became not only tears of grief but of gratitude for the things I was so thankful for.

I was still alive and blessed to have my family!

Our new life was a huge adjustment for all. Even in the midst of feeling lucky to be here, there were many challenges to face and barriers to work through for myself and my family.

Grieving the losses was one of them. The financial stability I worked so long and hard for and any future dream that I had been working towards for my family was gone. I realised that I had to start again and that's what I did!

It had not been easy living the life I was living, with all these changes and dreadful migraines that would leave me bed-bound for days on end, suffering a build-up of pressure and inflammation within my skull. Having a frontal sinus obliteration and the multiple metal objects now forming my new face, it still lacked its natural functions which proved to be an ongoing complication.

I was so thankful now to feel supported and not fall victim to the common lack of understanding and sometimes cruel, patronising, or harsh judgement by those I used to look to for support. They would say things like, "Shut up, I don't want to hear your BS. Be tough, brave it out, eat concrete, get over it. You wouldn't know what pain is; I'll show you pain, you have nothing to complain about, I been through much worse. Be grateful, you have nothing to cry about. It is your fault, not my problem. Think yourself lucky, you got a new face!" For so long, I smiled my way through painful silence, hiding away those parts of myself that needed to grieve just to make others feel better about themselves! Let me tell you, as I learnt to love myself and discovered my own self-worth, those friendships became short-lived – in fact, non-existent. I learnt to love myself enough to walk away from anything or anyone that doesn't feel right for me.

The space I made in doing this made room for people and things that are beautiful and complement my life in every way. I began to surround myself with people who supported my healing and my life. *They* became my soul family and walk alongside me with their love and support.

In that space, I came to accept that it was ok to grieve and grieving gave me the ability to accept. It was ok to let go: in fact, it was necessary. After all, the last eight years I had been through hell and back. I had a reason to feel sad living through all these experiences.

I realised at that point that it does not matter how strong and resilient we are and what adversities we overcome – we are only human, at least while here on Earth. We are not immune to grief. After any kind of loss, tragedy, or trauma, grieving is a healthy part of the recovery process. This needs to be acknowledged *as much as* the illness, injury, disability, trauma, or whatever you're dealing with. It is all a part of the acceptance of an experience. The process of grief and letting it go is integrating all those parts of ourselves that are meeting somewhere in the core of our being, connecting up and transforming to form this new you that comes out the other end of it all. That's the first step to finding the magic within yourself!

FEAR TO FREEDOM

Don't we, as humans, all want that magic?

You may have some questions rattling inside you right now, such as:

- Where to from here?
- How do I find the magic inside myself?
- After all I have been through, do I even have magic inside me?
- I go through so much pain, how could I feel anything else?

I understand. I may not understand your experience or your pain, I have not lived in your shoes, but I do want to support you in finding that place within yourself where you can answer all your own questions. Keep following me on this journey towards making this happen, and together we will open new doors and close unwanted, outdated, outgrown, or self-destructive doors that no longer serve you or your purpose!

You are not alone. I am here to help guide you to find the extra support you may be wanting in your life and empower you to create the life you want for yourself.

CHAPTER 8

SHIFTING FOCUS

My interpretation of god, may differ from your own,

This Great Spirit, a part of me, tells me I am never alone,

I am a child of the universe, this Great Love inside me,

leads the way, gracefully abiding me.

SHIFTING FOCUS

For all the kicks I got while I was down, as I rise, I thank you all for showing me how I got there. There is no one to blame or shame, as we are all weaving our own journey. My own need to give and my need to be accepted and loved rendered me powerless.

Now I want to show you why I kept kicking *myself* to the curb.

I had discovered there is no more debilitating disability than the mind. Our minds are the most powerful tool that we have! The mind can take us on two journeys: one will support our growth and progress and the other hinder our growth and progress.

We feel what we think about, we talk what we think about, we visualise what we think about, and in time, what are we going to manifest…?

What we are consistently thinking about!

I started to look at the patterns and actions within my own behaviour that had played out, always trying to help and give my all to others that would not take care of themselves, do for themselves, or help themselves. I was enabling them to just repeat their own behavioural patterns over and over. Meanwhile, my own had also become repetitive.

This behavioural pattern within friendships and relationships is known as co-dependency and that type of relationship is almost like an addiction in itself. It is an unhealthy pattern created inside ourselves that comes from learnt behaviours from a young age. This pattern becomes a habit and is played out at the expense of yourself and your happiness, as you are consistently relying on others for their approval and for your own sense of false happiness.

I realised it was *not ok* to take care of others to the point that it was hurting me. It was *not ok* to give everything away and leave myself nothing. It was *not ok* to be selfless when it was wearing me down. It was *not ok* to accept what others say or do to me if it damaged my self-worth or my body. It was *not ok* to stay down in the depths of despair, beating myself up or kicking myself about how I got there just because others had an opinion or lay heavy judgements upon my life!

I realised the really kind person that I thought I was had actually not been very kind to herself!

How were these behaviour patterns being kind to myself? I was not really being kind to anyone by allowing any of the behaviours to play out the way they had. As all the light bulbs turned on and lit up my mind, I began to put myself first! I began to feel it was ok to give myself the things I need or want. It is ok to be selfish if it is not hurting others. It is ok to have more than I need. It is ok what others think say or feel about that or about me as long as I don't accept it as my own worth...it is *all ok*! We cannot control what others do, feel, or say. However, we can take control of our own lives.

I finally surrendered and let go of my co-dependency patterns and felt a self-worth that I had not felt before.

This is where I learnt to really love myself: doing whatever I wanted to do, surrounding myself with what felt great! This is where I found my sweet spot.

I enrolled in further study of fitness and nutrition. I loved it and learnt to create my own health and fitness programs. I began doing weekend activities that I love, eating the foods that I love,

SHIFTING FOCUS

wearing clothes and accessories that I love, planting plants that I love looking at, surrounding myself with *all the things that I love*. I began working in a job that I loved: for someone that was told she would never work again, would not outlive two years, and struggled verbally to understand or put a whole sentence together many years prior, I felt so grateful to be working again. I draw on my own experiences when supporting and caring for others, finding ways to empower people in their day-to-day lives and work towards overcoming their challenges and achieve their goals, enabling them to better their own lives, find their magic, and ultimately, find their happiness.

This type of work too, comes with its challenges, but just like any other experience, when you always come back to the centre of why you're doing what you're doing, you come back to the purpose. The purpose is the motivation. The motivational reward *brings a sense of gratitude, greatness, and love!*

Do not get me wrong here: there are many moments, outside influences, stressful situations, and life experiences that come along and try to burst that bubble of love, but I always bring my focus back to what feels great.

Life has a way of throwing curve balls. We have many lessons to learn in order to grow and evolve.

We can always find ways to deal with the cards we are dealt – it makes us who we are!

To watch someone you love go through this is completely different to going through it yourself. To care for someone you love during times of partial or total debilitation means you are facing all the physical, mental, emotional, and financial challenges together. If you are sharing this journey with another, you may feel all the emotions they feel and a sense of helplessness that you are unable to take their pain or suffering away. Speaking from someone who has been on the other side, just having another person – whether it's a partner, family, friend, or carer – to walk beside you and support you in what you're going through, is what helps bring you back from the trauma of it all.

A SHIFT IN FOCUS

Enduring all kinds of trauma and starting again from nothing but a few pieces of furniture opened doors for new opportunities and many new beginnings. As I began thinking about all the positives, I realised there were so many, as my mind began to see the situation from a new perspective. Each day is something to be grateful for. I began shifting my focus towards the good stuff.

I was a walking miracle! I had overcome so much adversity. I found gratitude for more things than I can mention (that would be another book).

I realised how powerful the mind is. Our state of mind and the things we believe, the things we think about, and our attitudes, all trigger our feelings and greatly impact our health, wellbeing, and our environment.

When your life is tipped upside down and inside out, this is where the change begins. New seeds are ready to sow, to nurture, and grow!

Starting from nothing is the most beautiful opportunity to create a new life and all that you want for yourself: a life you want to live as

SHIFTING FOCUS

the person you want to be and a person you love being. This is the opportunity to build yourself from the ground up! Bring back the colour to your dreams and find your magic!

Staying positive in your thoughts strengthens your recovery when you have experienced any kind of trauma. It is important to mentally reframe your mind from the mind dysplasia that can happen from all kinds of experiences. Turning negative experiences into positive ones is a choice! If you have read this far into the book, my guess is you've already lived through some of your own challenging life experiences and know what that looks like and how it feels.

I want you to get a pen and paper or you can use the spaces provided. Sit for a moment and ask yourself a few simple questions. Be honest with yourself. This is just for you to see, no one else. These are your innermost feelings.

FACE *of* FAITH

Do you feel supported? _____

Would you like more support? _____

Are you totally happy with your lifestyle and environment? _____

Do you want to keep living as you are? _____

Do you feel truly happy in yourself? _____

Is there something that you would love to do that you are not currently doing? _____

What other things would you love to be doing or doing more of? ____

Is it possible for you to do these things? Are there other options to make it possible? _____

If so, what might those options be? _____

If you could start by changing one thing in your current circumstances, what would that be? _____

If you could change some of these things in your life, would you? ____

Why do you want this change? _____

Well, guess what? You can make changes to accommodate your wants, your needs, and the goals you may want to achieve! There may be some barriers or challenges that you may need to work through, but with the right supports in place to steer you towards what it is you want, you can achieve anything! Later, in Chapter 11, we will be exploring

SHIFTING FOCUS

this more and looking at setting goals and how to support yourself to achieve them.

It starts with making choices: choices that are right for you, that support you in every aspect of your life and how you want that to be. I know you have the mental strength to achieve *anything*. You have come this far, right? In saying that, have you ever stopped and praised yourself for how far you have come? Have you given yourself a pat on the back and celebrated your uniqueness and all the adversities you have faced up to this point?

Stop for a moment and tell yourself how proud you are of yourself for getting to where you are now and for picking up and reading this book. That, too, is taking time, energy, and effort towards yourself and your future. Thank yourself for every bit of courage it took to get to this point in your life. You are an amazing human being! I have not met you, but I know how much effort it takes to get to where you are now. I *know* you are extraordinary!

Feel how great it feels to be you! You really are awesome!!

Thank you for being you.

CHAPTER 9

MINDFUL MEMOIRS

If I don't tell you then who will,

If I don't make the shift then who will,

If I don't share my gift then who will,

If I share the secrets of my heart then you will,

If I make a change then you will,

If I give you the gifts I learnt then you will.

REHABILITATE

Management is the key to the mansion of rehabilitation. Learning to "manage" the symptoms of any condition, disability, injury, addiction, imbalance, or even our thought patterns, is the way to a healthy and happy life.

Be brave, move through the shadows, embrace the rain, use your feet that you were given to walk along your path. Even if it feels cold, damp, or dark at times, I promise you the sun will gravitate its light towards you and you will find the light within that warms your soul to its core.

Rehabilitation is the common goal, but we must first understand what we are rehabilitating from.

Regardless of our circumstances or what we are dealing with, whether it be short-term, long-term, or terminal, the goal toward our rehabilitation or recovery has a common thread that runs through all types of conditions. That is PAIN.

If you live with a disability, have sustained an injury, suffer an illness, terminal illness, or mental health condition, have experienced trauma, have a high-pressure lifestyle causing you to live in a constant state of stress, or are caring for a loved one, my guess is you have experienced pain. All of the above can cause pain of some kind and sometimes that pain is invisible. It is not always obvious that a person is suffering pain. When the physical aspect is healed or hidden, it can bring about a silent suffering.

If you are one of those people, there are many ways you can take control of your wellbeing and not let your experience control you.

This begins with educating yourself on every aspect of what is happening to you physically, mentally, and emotionally, and exploring all aspects of yourself and your experience in order to begin your healing process, holistically, from the inside out.

Your experience does not own you: you own it and *you own you!*

Let's begin this exploration here and learn to take care of your needs in every way. You can do this by opening the doors of support you may need to be able to work through your own experience and come out the other side, happier and able to live life to the fullest.

At this point, you may be saying to yourself, "I can't change anything or do what I want to do. This woman has no idea about my pain." You're absolutely right: I don't have any idea about your pain, what you are going through, or what you live with, but I certainly understand what it is like to experience my own as I have shared with you. I am living proof that you can live life on the other side of all that. And you will, if that is what you choose.

Let's explore what pain is. What is the experience of pain? What type is it? Where does pain come from? How is it felt? Everyone has a different description of pain and it has many types and forms. But I think we can all agree it is a sensation that is extremely unpleasant.

The scientific and medical research I discovered during my years of attending rehabilitation groups whilst being treated under my pain management team shows us that pain is a signal from the brain. Nerve fibres carry the pain signals or impulses to the brain, then the brain sends signals back with a physical sensory warning to inform your body that if we touch the stove again, our skin will melt. These sensory signals affect us physically and emotionally, letting us know something is wrong.

People without limbs can still experience a neuropathic pain in the limb that they no longer have, which is known as phantom limb pain. Where there is an old injury that no longer exists we can also experience neuropathic pain! There are various prescription medications and techniques available out there that can assist in switching off that part of the brain that sends the signals.

We know there is a reason behind physical pain, but how about the emotional kind? Can our heart ache? Not the organ that pumps blood around the body, but our heart centre, our spiritual heart, the core of our being. Of course: we are human and not immune to grief. It is a natural human occurrence. Each of us is unique and has a certain threshold for being able to manage physical and emotional experiences. We are always going to have "good and bad" days. Those days we call "bad" days can help us to learn more about ourselves and what our needs are, signalling us to connect with what is happening inside of us and integrate those unintegrated parts of ourselves. As we do this, we build up our threshold, becoming stronger, more self-aware, and restoring balance back into our lives.

BARRIERS

"…If you can't fly then run

If you can't run then walk,

If you can't walk then crawl,

whatever you do, you have to keep moving forward…"

MARTIN LUTHER KING

I was writing this book for a ridiculous length of time – seven years, in fact! My journaling kept slipping its way down to the bottom of my priority list. My tribe expanded over time and life just kept happening for all of us, each with our own path of learning. Even as I became healthier and happier, there have been many barriers and challenges along the way. The most important one for me to overcome was learning to take the time to care for myself in ways that supported my healing and made me happy. ♥

The great lesson here is "life happens," and no matter what, you have to make yourself, your needs, and *what you want for yourself* a priority. You are *your* responsibility and you owe it to yourself to make *yourself* happy!

Finding your inner magic and happiness, in the midst of enduring pain from any condition is achievable. I want to help you achieve that feeling of happiness within.

I cannot express enough, it does not matter what trauma you have been through or whatever condition or circumstances you have. You

MINDFUL MEMOIRS

can move forward, you can change, and adapt. You can achieve and experience happiness!

We are about to look at some mindful memoirs on managing challenges and insightful ways to find your way back to yourself. Remember, you are not alone on this path. I and many others have been there.

In saying that, I tell you they are not just words I write. I only use words to express what I feel in my heart. I understand your suffering. No, I do not live in your body or feel what you feel, and it may not be the same as my pain or experiences, and our journeys may differ greatly, but I understand the challenges you face and how difficult it can be to move forward from a place of total fear or despair.

You may have a condition that has developed, improved, or deteriorated over time that requires change in your life: a change in your thinking, your attitude, and the activities you normally do. It could be that you need a total reassessment of what your abilities are now. What worked before may not work anymore. This does not mean that this disability is totally disabling, it just means you may not be able to do the things you used to do in the same way. Or perhaps you are wanting to up the ante, if you have improved and healed something that you never thought possible, and may be needing new goals with more stimulus?

As I say, the things that mattered before may not matter anymore. Why fret, be angry, or upset at what is no longer? Surrender it and find new ways that support your growth. We shine when focused on what we can achieve.

Let go of what no longer fulfils you and explore new things you can enjoy, or enjoy what you have always done in an alternate way.

Our next step is identifying barriers and learning to look at them from a different perspective. Let's say we look at those barriers and see them as just a challenge, instead of an impossible obstacle that is in our way?

We face and overcome challenges every day. Barriers are not disabling, they are not debilitating. It does not mean we can't do something and will never be able to enjoy the experience of it. It just means we may be unable to do that task or enjoy that experience in the same way others do, or experience it in the same way we may have been able to before. We just need to find another way of doing or enjoying whatever it is.

Some of these barriers may be around our actual condition we live with, but the pain we feel may also be our own negative attitudes: if you feel victimised with so much blame and shame that you refuse to take responsibility for yourself, it may be your thought patterns, or beliefs, or the lack of supporting yourself whilst expecting others to do it all. It may be cultural, or the stigma or attitudes towards your condition, which can impact on your self-esteem and ability to achieve. It may be your fears and being afraid to move forward and achieve what you want for yourself, in case you fail or succeed? There may be fear of success or being rejected. There may be stress factors.

Even stress becomes toxic. Stress felt in the body causes us to breathe shallow breaths and release a brain chemical known as cortisol. If this continues over long periods, the imbalance of chemicals in the body causes illness and disease in the body!

When imbalance occurs, we go back to what is comfortable, to what we know, to what we think makes us feel good, even if we know it is for a short time, a quick fix, and gives us the feel-good sensation for a short time! This is how addiction occurs. This could be a good thing if it is fresh air, exercise, and healthy food we are addicted too! On the other hand, the quick fixes are often unhealthy ones, including excessive substance abuse, excessive eating, excessive shopping, gambling, or finding ways to self-medicate. Then follows a destructive pattern, causing more stress, more chemicals released in the brain, and so on. This is not really solving the problem, it is a cycle.

Some of these we may think are normal and accepted. I'm certainly not saying there's anything wrong with things we enjoy in moderation, but done to excess it just keeps us living in an unhealthy pattern of existence.

Enduring pain is one thing but to "suffer" pain, addiction, self-loathing, blaming, shaming or harbouring guilt, leaves your dimmer switch on low. Not feeling good about yourself is not a way to live. It might be comfortable or a little less than comfortable, so why settle for that type of comfort when you can feel happy, turn that light up bright, and feel the magic within you, no matter what?

Connect with the unique amazing person that you are.

Learning to manage our fears and feelings brings you halfway home. Embrace your fear, own it, and keep walking forward! Let us step out of that comfort zone a little and delve into *you*!

Stop for a moment to explore some of your own barriers, fears, stresses, or obstacles you have that are holding you back from your happiest life. Remember, this is about you and for you – you don't need to share this with anyone, unless you would like to. It is helpful to share, but totally up to you. We are delving more into finding the right supports for you later.

Take a pen and your notepad or again feel free to use the space provided here.

What are some of the daily challenges you have? _____

What are some of your stress factors or environmental factors that may be causing you stress? _____

What are the barriers you are up against? _____

What do you feel afraid of? _____

Where in your body can you feel it? _____

Are there triggers for you? _____

As you begin to answer these questions about what is happening for you, you will feel more self-aware. As you become more in touch with yourself, begin to recognise what increases the tension and feelings of fear and what decreases these anxious feelings inside your body.

During my life, not only have I been faced with my own barriers, but also challenges working among the disability, vision impaired, and mental health sectors. I also witnessed and supported others to work through theirs. Among my many caring roles as a community worker I mentioned in earlier chapters, I worked at the blind association in Victoria. I had many clients who were partially or completely vision impaired. I witnessed firsthand the effects of day-to-day challenges and worked through ways to enable people without sight. I want to share with you some examples of insightful ways you can overcome some of these challenges.

MINDFUL MEMOIRS

A person who is born vision impaired or becomes completely vision impaired faces many barriers here, which are challenging. The people I worked with were multi-talented and taught me a thing or two about how to see without seeing. That was an eye-opener for me and I am a fully sighted person! I also learnt not to take the simplest of things for granted.

A vision impaired person cannot see to be able to read their own mail, read books, the newspaper, menus at restaurants, take their own medications, see their phone to be able to call someone in the event of an emergency, to fold their clothes and put them away, to buy groceries, to cook a meal without issues around meal prep and safety, to shower themselves, go to the toilet, to see the keyboard to use a computer, to listen to music or watch TV, see street signs on a walk, put a CD in the stereo, connect Bluetooth to listen to music devices, see cars going by on the road, drive themselves to and from work or around to social events, or go out for lunch. So how do they keep themselves safe in and outside the home, living in darkness? There are hundreds of challenges for a person without sight!

Facing day-to-day challenges like these can cause multiple issues, depression, anxiety, safety issues, fear, isolation, disconnection from society, loneliness, lack of self-confidence, suicidal tendencies, and many more. But this book is about problem-solving, so let us unpack this and have a look at examples of how support can be offered and how things that can be done differently, to stay engaged, and enjoy living a healthy and happy life!

They may need to catch taxis or public transport with the use of a cane or a guide dog after support training to help use the guide dog. A support worker visiting regularly can assist with groceries, regular appointments, community activities, and household tasks that may be difficult. Containers, pots and pans, cups, bowls, and all kitchen items should be marked with bumps, ridges, or something that can be felt before the full line. Everything stacked in familiar places to establish familiarity within the home. Computer programs with audio that reads everything and sends messages to mobiles. An emergency device should be worn around the neck to signal to family, friends, or emergency services to send for help quickly when needed. As you can see, there many ways to support a vision impaired person to overcome challenges.

How about a person who is quadriplegic?

An inspiring story that I want to share about a client I had over 25 years ago when I was working in the field as an attendant "in-home carer." A man I attended on a few evenings each week; a man that I am going to name "Extraordinary."

Extraordinary was in his 50s when I met him. He was quadriplegic from the neck down and needed 24-hour round-the-clock in home care. He was unable to move in his chair or do anything for himself, although he had mouth sticks with all different devices on the ends of them, to be able to turn pages in books, flick computer buttons and buttons on his chair. I was warned by co-workers how cranky, difficult, and quick to anger he was. The daily notes carers and nurses wrote in his communication diary were always unpleasant.

My first experience caring for him, I approached him as my usual chatty self and he acted the way everyone said. My notes probably did not look any different to all the other daily notes in his communication book. Immediately, I understood why I was warned. Over the months, I began sharing with him a few of my not-so-nice experiences and how they changed my life and helped me to become more self-aware.

MINDFUL MEMOIRS

Extraordinary began to talk openly on each visit about how and when he became quadriplegic at a very young age and the many years of surgical interventions and the time he spent in and out of hospital requiring ongoing care for the rest of his life. I probed him about the things that made him feel happy, and learnt that he enjoyed learning to paint with brushes using his mouth, as this is the only part of his body he could use. He did a few oil paintings on canvas when he was in his 20s, which were displayed on his loungeroom wall. But due to ongoing medical intervention, he did not continue to pursue art. On each visit, I took pieces of art, pictures, writings, inspiring quotes, and a few books for him to ponder. We spent many hours discussing the things that took his interest.

He began painting again. He became happier in himself and lovely to spend time with. His day-to-day notes from carers and nurses began to reflect the change in him! I was amazed at his talent and ability to paint such beautiful pictures with sticks in his mouth and not a great deal of movement in his neck. He had to put the brushes down to pick up the mouth pieces that enabled his chair to move directions to then add the smallest of strokes to the canvas. His paintings were making their way to the walls around his small apartment. I watched his frustration ease and his patience and happiness bloom as he painted more. I finished up working with Extraordinary.

Around a year later, the company asked if I could do one daytime shift with him as he had requested to see me. I drove to a place that was not the same place he lived before and when I walked in, he had a huge smile on his face. His happiness was beaming from within. He began telling me he had continued painting and had his paintings put into local galleries and entered art competitions, extending to larger galleries around Australia and found a new bigger and better apartment for himself! I was laughing and crying at the same time that he had achieved this amazing accomplishment and was becoming famous for his art work.

Extraordinary. What else could I call him? He was extraordinary! How do you think he achieved his goals with all the barriers and day-to-day challenges he faced?

He shifted his focus, changed his attitude toward life, began to believe in himself and focused on what he wanted to achieve – not on what had happened to him or what he could not do!

He was a quadriplegic who could not move a limb or do anything for himself; who needed to be fed with a spoon, hoisted in and out of bed and to use the bathroom; and yet, he was still able to enjoy his life and follow his dreams, becoming an inspiration and successful! It took focus, a strong belief in himself, and encouraging support from people around him.

MINDFUL MEMOIRS

HOLISTIC CARE AND SUPPORT

The key word that has been repeated throughout these pages is *support, support, support*! There can never be enough: bathe and surround yourself in it and the people that care for you, but remember to support yourself too. Support is needed in order to thrive. It is your care, so is important to have carers, a program, a health plan, or whatever it may be, to support what you want. As we move forward into the next chapters, we will be looking at lots of awesome ideas, activities, and alternatives to get you thinking about the goals you may want to add and how you are going to achieve them. You might already be looking at the changes you want to make with the previous questions we went through: the changes that will need to be made along the way to suit your life, your cultural beliefs, your ability, physical changes, your age, stage of recovery, your environment, and your circumstances, as all those things change and play a factor. Nothing ever stays the same, change is the only constant we have. Embrace the changes and challenges along the way. It is your journey: let's make the most of it!

Who makes these decisions? Who chooses what is right for you? *You* of course! Why? Because, only you know what is right for you; only you know what feels good for you and what makes you happy. It is your life and your journey – no one else's. Your journey is only felt by you, only experienced by you. This is where you get to own all of you, taking back any power you gave to others to create or control your life. This is where you create the future you have dreamed about, living your best life the way you want. You are not "just" the patient or a number – you are on a journey of your life!

Let's explore a few things we need to think about when considering making decisions about your recovery or your future, regardless of your circumstances. Is it short-term, long-term, or life-long management?

FACE *of* FAITH

Is it for a client or patient/person you care for that may not be able to make any decisions for themselves? What else do we need, other than a team of fabulous specialists, therapists, and ongoing appointments to support our medical needs? If you want to heal from the inside out, we need to put things in place that work for you, taking care of every part of you from the inside out! We need to create a support base, from medicinal care to caring for the body, mind, and spirit.

Here come my warmest words: *"holistic care."* ♥ I get butterflies in my belly and a smile on my face just thinking about this.

What is holistic care? I am sure most people have heard of this type of care, but what does it really mean? Holistic care is caring for the whole self, not just the physical body. It is caring for the mind, the emotional aspects, and our spiritual self, working on our body, mind, and soul!

This is where we discover all our needs and take care of every one of them. It involves focusing on your healing, what works, and what makes you feel awesome about yourself. Have faith and hope in yourself. Believe from the core of your thinking that you are always healing. "Fight for yourself" as you would fight for someone you love. Find hope in your recovery and in your life. Your recovery is not just medicinal; it's learning to really love and care for yourself. Self-love is the most powerful medicine there is! This is your journey and your recovery. Do what feels right and great for you and you will find the road back to yourself and connect to the innermost magical parts of who you are. ♥

How do we get holistic care? To treat every aspect of yourself, you need to think deeply about all your needs and wants, your challenges, your goals, your aspirations, inspirations, and what you might need to achieve them. Then, make a plan! If you feel a little overwhelmed by this, have a look at how far you've come already and how resilient you are. We have already begun this process by answering the previous questions. You are doing amazing! I believe in you! Believe in yourself and back yourself 100%.

I know what it feels like to be on the other side of trauma with feelings of doubt and not knowing what's going to happen. But I know that doing all you can to love and care for yourself will bring you back home, to a beautiful place within that is full of love and magic! You won't look back with regret, only gratitude for yourself, regardless of your circumstances.

After I was told I had less than two years to live and in those years I would suffer a fast deterioration with my motor skills being severely impacted from the infectious bone disease eating away through to brain matter, the fear I felt impacted my ability to heal. I continued to attend all my medical appointments, meetings, and the Chinese Medicine practitioner. He had me working on my physical health, my physical body, my mind, and spiritual practises to heal myself. For some years, each day, I would drink four litres of wheatgrass to neutralise acid within my body, take 15 little black pills containing Chinese herbs for my condition, high doses of Himalayan salt, zinc, magnesium, very high doses of vitamin C (10,000 mg a day), some form of physio exercise, yoga, or super long walks, and each week I would attend one therapeutic activity, alternating and exploring all kinds of alternative therapies, from Bowen therapy, massage, hydrotherapy, spa therapy, acupuncture, alternative healing therapies, meditation circles to full moon healing ceremonies. Over time, I discovered what worked for me and wrote up my own plan and what I needed to do to support myself so that I would stick to that plan. I was treating my whole self holistically.

During the process, I became aware of my thought processes affecting my emotions and my actions. I became so self-aware that I could feel exactly what was happening inside me and began using my mind and the energy source within myself that I tapped into to heal my body. I went to extremes of visualising shooting powerful white holes in the black cloud of the illness I had inside my skull. That's right, you heard it, the illness "I had" actually disappeared completely to scar tissue. It took many years but treating my whole self with all these great tools and really loving myself created a healthy mind, a healthy body, and a happy spirit! If our mind and body can manifest illness, we can manifest health and happiness too.

CHAPTER 10

FIND YOUR MAGIC

Smile back even when being frowned upon

Get back up every time you fall

As you walk into the unknown

Awaken… remember who you are

Love yourself unconditionally

In a world full of conditions.

FIND YOUR MAGIC

SELF-NURTURE AND THE PATH TO HAPPINESS

Finding something that works (and works effectively), that helps you to live your best life is what is important. Why? Because *you* are important.

In the previous questions, we looked at some of the barriers and day-to-day challenges you may be facing and some changes you may want to make. Now, we are going to look at the extra support you might need to achieve this in your life. In exploring what you want, you are opening your mind to possibilities and creating a sense of self-awareness before working on the ways in which you can achieve this.

In this chapter, we are exploring lots of different ideas to assist you in putting together a creative plan that will support you in achieving your ideal life. This is the life that *you* want for yourself: your happiest life!

Becoming proactive in your life and your own care is as important as having carers and specialists caring for you. It is really up to us, as individuals, to maintain a certain standard of living to maintain our own health and happiness. We can be guided to do this or that and have support to help us achieve it, but we need to get up each day and do the work toward achieving this *ourselves*. I know it can be challenging. I have put in the hard yards, so I get it! That's why I am breaking all this down into a way that is helpful to support you now to do the same.

Listen to the nagging voice inside you that is begging to be heard, telling you what you really want for yourself. That inner voice may be harping on at you for exercise, a healthier diet, a change in habits that may be good, bad, or indifferent. A fun activity, a change of scenery, a move into a larger or smaller home because the one you're in just doesn't fit or feel right for your situation anymore. It may be a holiday to a place you have been wanting to go to, or something you have been playing out in your imagination! Now is the time to manifest what's in your creative mind's eye. *I know you can.*

Do things because you want to, not because it is a form of habit or you think you should. You would not tell your best friend to do something they do not like doing.

Clean up your old ways of thinking that you can't do this or that because of this or that. Mentally reframe your mind into a healthier direction. Challenge yourself!

As we have been discussing throughout these pages, we may need to work within certain limitations, but if you want to go to the moon and back, focus on your target, use the powerful intent you were born with, and MAKE IT HAPPEN! That in itself might take more than a few goals and an entire lifetime to achieve, but the point I am trying to make is whatever you want, work towards it, and back yourself all the way!

We must keep taking simple steps each day towards taking care of *ourselves*, taking care of your own wants, needs, and your own goals. With your new awareness, you can adopt healthier behaviours that support you. Engage with yourself on every level, become your own best friend, and treat yourself the way you would your best friend.

Here is another exercise for you to do. These questions need only simple yes or no answers. However, it is totally up to you in what you want to add. It is your own evaluation. These are just to help you become aware of what is happening for you around support and to help you think about what you want in your plan we are working towards in

FIND YOUR MAGIC

the next chapters. It helps to unpack all these questions before heading into goal setting to help you become more self-aware and look at what may be lacking in order to work towards what you want for yourself.

Take your time feeling yourself out here. Really get a feel for what you may want to change about your current circumstances and how you can work towards that.

Get yourself your favourite drink, something sexy – you are worth it! Grab a pen and your notebook or use the space provided to write your answers.

Are you getting your needs met? _____

Do you feel heard in what you need for yourself? _____

Are your supporters, family, or carers responding to what you need or want? _____

Are you feeling supported? _____

Do you have choice and control or someone to advocate for what you need in your support network? _____

Does this FEEL right for you? _____

Are you feeling frustrated with certain areas of your life and need more support in those areas? _____

If you could change things about the way you are being supported, what might those changes be about the current support you are receiving?
_____

If you haven't already put thought into all the other previous questions because you were so excited and just wanted to keep reading to find out what happened in the end, well, as you know life happens – there is never an end, only to this book. I will be writing another one after this and maybe another one after that. But for now, it is the time to start asking yourself those few questions to find out where you are at with your own life.

We are about to explore a few different and alternative forms of therapy, various tools, creative ideas, mindful strategies, and other fun stuff you can choose from and use as part of your holistic care plan. These can be used in conjunction with any medical intervention or recovery program, but always check with your team of specialists first!

There are many ways we can enjoy ourselves, but again, it is all about finding what brings enjoyment to you. While reading through these ideas, I want you to really take notice of what jumps out at you, what makes you feel excited and jump up saying, "That's me, I really want to do that!" We want to bring fun back into the equation. We just need to find the things you are able to do that make you feel great and then spend more time doing them. Everything that makes us happy is a therapy! Let's just explore what works for you, making it fun and therapeutic.

Invite activities into your life that make you feel great, do activities that lift you to a happier place inside yourself, then do more of what makes you feel happy. Then keep doing more. *And repeat!*

When you are doing activities that make you feel good, the glands throughout your body produce chemicals that are known as our "happy" hormones. The feeling produced by these chemicals makes us feel fantastic and alive with vibrancy. There are many things we can do to trigger those happy hormones. Many of them are therapeutic, that we can make a part of our everyday life. Some you may already be doing. If you are and it makes you feel awesome, make the time for yourself to do more of it!

Get creative in your activities, indulge the senses. I want to help you find healthier alternatives to strive for, to find what makes you tick, and what makes you get excited to get up each morning!

Let's do it!

During this process, educating yourself on new things may spark new interests or new ideas for things you would love to add to your plan we are working towards, but you may be saying to yourself, "I just don't have the time for this." The new things you might want you may not have the space for. Or you may feel physically or mentally unable to do it. This is where you really need to look at what's holding you back, and work through those challenges to prioritise what is important and of great value to you. We can always find solutions. This may mean letting go of some outdated ideas or goals or things that no longer hold value for you and no longer give you the pleasure it once did and do not serve the life you are living now. Look outside the box and view things from a fresh, new perspective.

You might want to take notes in your notebook or highlight below the things that jump out at you and take your interest, so we can research further for the plan you will make for yourself in the next chapter.

EDUCATE YOURSELF

Gain awareness and expand your knowledge about what you want to know more about. If something takes your interest, check out your local library. Even reading "how to" books is a learning curve or check out what your local education institutions have to offer. Knowledge is empowering; to know is to grow!

I also encourage you to learn as much as you can about any condition you may have. Educating yourself helps you further understand your own needs and reduces fear and stigma around it all. It is self-empowering to give yourself the information you need to understand what you are dealing with and how you can best take care of yourself. There are many factors that can impact or improve your recovery. If you are caring for another, you can educate yourself on their condition to understand what they may be dealing with also.

The more we arm ourselves with self-awareness and expand our knowledge, we open doors for ourselves that support change in our lifestyle. The more support we put in place, the more supported we feel to achieve our goals, the more we achieve, the happier we feel, the more we heal!

DECLUTTER YOUR LIFE

There is nothing like a good clean out of all the things that no longer serve a purpose in making our lives a happy one.

The clutter in our homes, our vehicles, our offices, our garages, our pantries, and our fridges is a reflection of what is also going on in our minds. This means we can't do one without the other. Decluttering

FIND YOUR MAGIC

is a process of cleaning up our entire lives, from our homes to what we fill our pantries with, to what we are thinking about.

Clutter is disorganisation and chaotic, which can cause more stress! If you eliminate some of that clutter, you will feel more organised and less stressed just from that act alone.

It can seem overwhelming to declutter or try to organise a whole lot of stuff at once. Do not attempt to do it all at once! Pick something that bothers you the most and start there, maybe a drawer that is full of unused junk that you just can't find anything in or doesn't shut properly. We all have junk drawers from hell, but they are actually handy drawers when you know what is in them, and when they are opening and closing properly! Or start with a kitchen cupboard that is so full everything falls out when you open it and you only use one fifth of the stuff in there. Or your pantry: you might want to start being more mindful about what you are eating, instead of filling your cupboard with easy quick fixes that are cluttering your pantry (and your body too). Or start with your wardrobe that has so many items of clothing you can't find anything to wear, or you don't know what to wear because you can't see what's in there, or you don't like wearing what is in there anymore anyway, so why keep it?

Get a box (or 12!) and start organising them into charity boxes, family giveaway boxes, and bin boxes. No one wants your rubbish. I give at least a trailer of stuff away yearly. You would literally be starting from scratch if I got my hands in there. In the past, I have helped clients who hoard and they will tell you that I am ruthless when it comes to a clean out. Do not invite me over!

If you're not sure if you want to keep certain things, here are a few questions to ask yourself:

1. Does it make me feel happy or great about myself?
2. Does that item support me in some way, physically or mentally?
3. Does it fit?
4. Do I use it?

If you answer yes to more than two of these questions, keep it. If you have answered no to each question, pick a box to put it in. Go on, just do it. Throw it in a box, you don't need it. It is that simple!

If this is something you need to do, we will work on that in your plan. You will feel so much better for clearing out the stuff you don't want or need, stuff that just takes up space in your home and in your life. Someone else will benefit from your unwanted things and most importantly *you* will benefit because you are making all this space now for things you do want – things that you love!

SELF-CARE

Let us look at self-care and what that really means. Are we caring for ourselves the best way we could be? Do you look after all aspects of yourself the way you would your best friend or your pets?

You may be the carer or the one with the condition and have time constraints and or limitations? That is ok – you still deserve to feel great about yourself!

Become your favourite person and treat yourself as though you are the most important person in the world. Be kind and loving to yourself, nurture yourself in any way you enjoy, really putting the emphasis on the "feel good" stuff.

FIND YOUR MAGIC

Let's explore ways we can improve our self-care habits and begin our journey of truly nurturing the whole self.

What are you eating? Are you getting the exercise you need? What are you drinking? How much are you drinking? When was the last time you had a health check with your doctor? Do you take care of your daily personal care needs? What about your feet? Or your muscles? Our feet and our bodies work every day carrying us around. Treat yourself to a full body or foot remedial massage or foot spa – they are not expensive and are like a short time lapse of being in *heaven*! You may not have had your hair done for a while or get creative doing your own hair, have fun with it.

Wear the clothes you love to wear, wear your most comfortable shoes, no matter what they look like. Does it matter that much what other people say about how we like to dress? Or does it matter more how you feel about yourself? That's the only thing here that matters: how we feel about how we look. What styles and colours we wear impacts how we feel. Try wearing blue or green when feeling angry, it has a calming effect. Try wearing something bright when you feel flat and need a boost of happiness. It is empowering. Dress in whatever makes you feel sexy!

NUTRITION

It is important to clean up our diets if we want to feel as healthy as possible. If we have a healthy diet, we are supporting and contributing to a healthy body.

What we consume impacts on our entire system and determines a big part of our health and vitality. What we put in our bodies can hinder or support us. There is a saying, "We are what we eat." Take a close look at what you are eating and drinking, and ask yourself: is it nourishing your cells? Is it making you feel good? Is what you are consuming daily giving you energy, vitality, and longevity?

Nourishing the body with nutritious foods gives us energy, helps us function, maintains a healthy body, and helps us to live a healthier life. If you need assistance with learning about nutrition and how to maintain a healthy diet, you could add this into your plan and educate yourself further on nutrition under the Australian Dietary guidelines. If you are interested in learning more, book in to see a nutritionist or dietician to assist in educating and supporting yourself with healthy lifestyle changes.

I attended a nutrition workshop many years ago. The hosts shared research and facts on scientific evidence on those living in the blue zones: Okinawa in Japan, Sardinia in Italy, Loma Lind in California, and Ikaria in Greece. These people live extraordinarily long and healthy lives, being socially engaged and active, living on plant-based diets, with soy, nuts, legumes etc… all free from harsh chemicals, preservatives, and additives. On the other end of the spectrum, 70% of deaths in the Western world are caused by preventable disease. Some of the evidence showed disease due to ill-health from highly processed foods. These scientific studies show that genetics are only responsible for up to 10% of disease risk, while 90% of disease is caused by lifestyle.

ACTIVITY SPORT EXCERCISE

Exercise releases all kinds of "happy, feel good" chemicals within your body and these chemicals make us feel exhilarated and alive. They help relieve the symptoms of stress, pain, and tension in the body. Any kind of movement supports an improvement on your health, mental health, strength, fitness, and flexibility. There is no better high than our own body's natural high! It is magical.

Is there a particular activity, sport, or other form of exercise you would like to start doing or can you do more of one you are already doing? Depending on your level of ability, age, and stage, for you this could mean participating in an activity or engaging by attending sport games to watch the sport.

There are endless leisurely and fun activities to choose from: walking, running, gym, strength training, dance class, martial arts, swimming, hydrotherapy, physiotherapy, hot sauna/spa, kayaking, bike riding, riding horses, riding for the disabled, yoga, Pilates, tai chi, tennis, or ball games. There are many local team sports around if team sports takes your interest. You may want to speak with a physiotherapist or professional personal trainer to help you decide on a fitness program as hard and fast, or as gentle and slow, as you like. It can be tailored to suit your needs. Even laying in the water at a hydrotherapy pool can be amazing. Do yourself a favour and make one or more of these a part of your life.

There are no excuses. If you are time-poor, do a little less of something that you don't enjoy so much and use that time doing something for you, something that excites your senses. You will feel so much better for it.

Just so you know, for those of you saying right now, "I can't:" I've been told I can't do things many times, but I did them anyway! Find what you *can* do and what suits your needs and circumstances.

REST REJUVENATE RECOVER

Breaks in life are a must! A day here and there relaxing and switching off from everything restores balance. Weekends away and weeks away once in a while are a great way to break up the day-to-day routine in our lives.

On a day-to-day basis, short breaks and cups of our favourite drink, tea, coffee, latte, or chai over a long day can be as refreshing as a holiday to the nearest beach. We need to rejuvenate and refresh ourselves regularly.

This can be challenging for high achievers who want to get the most out of every minute of each and every day. I know how a busy schedule can keep us running on adrenaline and that excess adrenaline energy makes us feel like we have the energy to keep pushing on all day, but it is unhealthy to force our bodies to live in a constant state of stress. Science shows that staying in that energy activates the fight or flight response, which then releases more chemicals within the body. This is ok in short bursts if we need to run from a bear or fight a bear but being stuck in that state over a long period of time forms illness within the body. Then we receive the news of the illness, creating more stress and so on. You can see where this leads to: nowhere pleasant, and certainly not to happiness.

When we take a step back, it rejuvenates us and relaxes our entire body, from the brain to the toes, including the adrenal glands. When we do something nice for ourselves, our body loves it and will thank us in return by feeling refreshed and happy.

There are many ways we can take breaks. Enjoy a lunch or dinner with friends or family. Book in for a massage, spoil yourself with a day spa facial or body treatment. Take yourself out to the cinemas or have a day at home. Have a movie marathon day. Keep your curtains drawn and do nothing. Pack a picnic and go sit at the nearest water's edge, or read a good book in the sunshine. Buy a hammock and put it out under your favourite tree: lay in it even for 15 minutes and I promise you will want to stay there a lot longer than that! Hammocks are the best ever relaxation.

It is actually fun and revitalising to destress and do nothing! If you able, go for a weekend away somewhere you would like to explore. Give yourself permission to take a break, rest, and rejuvenate.

MINDFUL MEDITATION PRACTISE

Here, we are exploring healthier ways to manage stress. The best way to calm the mind is through relaxation, as we just looked at. Research shows relaxation actively releases stress and tension and lowers inflammation in the body. This is a much happier place to be heading towards.

Meditation is a relaxing technique for your whole body. It calms your mind as you focus on your breath and breathing deeply while slowing down the breath. This can be done in many ways, through sitting, laying down, with the use of yoga postures, hand gestures known as mudras, or repetitive words chanted in what's called a mantra. You can listen to guided meditation with music to help you relax into this space. It can help to have something to focus on when you're beginning, such as sound, music, a word, a mantra, a candle flame, or a picture. I have created a self-loving meditation for you in the last chapter of the book to begin or expand on your journey of mindful meditation.

During meditation practise, you can focus on one or more of your energy centres. There are many of these, but modern meditation practise tends to focus on the seven main energy centres known as chakras. There is a diagram in the last chapter if you are interested in exploring this further.

Crystals are another beautiful addition to your mindful practise, connecting you to their powerful energies and earthly vibrations. Crystals are another way to get in touch with the more hidden elements and energies of our Mother Earth. There are many different types and can be used in conjunction with your chakras and meditation practises or carried around with you. Choose the ones that give you comfort, the ones you can feel their vibrational and healing qualities. I have them placed around my home, in pot plants, in the garden and everywhere spreading their vibrations and beautiful energies.

ALTERNATE THERAPIES

There are many alternative therapies which are also known as complementary therapies that are also great for the body mind and soul. These tune us inward, bringing a closer connection to ourselves. I am sure there are at least more than one of these you might like to try and once you find something that excites your senses, make it a part of your plan. Here is a list of all kinds of alternate therapies to jump online and research in your own time. You may find something that works well for you! Remedial massage, Reiki healing, Bowen therapy, body balancing, hypnosis, kinesiology, acupuncture, flower essence therapy, Chinese Medicine or herbalism, naturopathy, and any others you may come across in your own research. Always check with your team of specialists to see what may or may not be effective and appropriate to complement any medical intervention or treatment in process.

FIND YOUR MAGIC

ARTISTIC THERAPY

The use of creation and colour is another way to enhance our senses and tap into that inner space of awesomeness.

You don't need to be an artist or crafty to create. I have never considered myself an artist but somehow when I get creative and zone into whatever idea comes to mind, I create something from nothing: a painting, a poem, amazing photos, this book, a beautiful garden, the best flavoured meal, an exercise program, designing and decorating a peaceful room, or making gifts. I just love creating. It is fun, therapeutic, and feels awesome!

There are many forms of art. Using colours and assorted materials and textures, you can create illustrations, calligraphy, writing, pottery, painting, designing, craft creations, knitting, crocheting, photography, music, and so much more. If you feel inspired, take up an art class, write your own book, or pick up a pencil and draw or decorate your home with all the things you love.

MUSIC AND SOUND

Music, sound, and its vibration soothes us and makes us feel great. There's nothing else like dancing or pumping out an exercise class to your favourite music. You can just listen to music you love or you may want to learn to play your own instrument or love singing. Singing is super powerful: smash out a tune to your favourite songs. Just do it.

Get lessons if you want to be a pro at it. If you really enjoy music, it is time to turn it up, sing out loud, or learn to play that instrument, feel the music move you. It changes your vibe!

Another form of sound that can be used is Tibetan chanting or throat singing. It is a spiritual discipline and a very powerful healing tool. It is one of the most amazing things I have felt. If you're up for something different and you want to feel that vibrational dance from within you, search your local area for a sound healing workshop. I will also be offering a workshop for this in the future.

CREATING A SUPPORT NETWORK

There are many ways to build a network within your own life: support groups, family gatherings, get togethers, social events, business meetings, social media, text messaging, catching up over the phone, lunches with friends, and a regular date night with your partner.

You may need further support with the assistance of a case manager who can help advocate for you. There are also well-known agencies that provide funding packages for the elderly, youth, or those living with a permanent condition who require extra support. Check out my Facebook Face of Faith Wellness business page @faceoffaithwellness for further information on what further support we offer and other services that may be available to you.

The purpose of creating this for yourself is staying connected and to surround yourself with the community of support that helps you achieve what it is you want for yourself and assists with making this more affordable.

FIND YOUR MAGIC

Remember that how you feel and what you want matters! Here, you will become proactive in advocating for yourself. Speak up for your needs or the needs of the person you are caring for. There is always room for improvements and change. Change is healthy.

COUNSELLING SUPPORT

We have explored grief in an earlier chapter and we understand it is a natural response to a loss or major change of any kind. It is coming to terms with what has changed in your life. This can take time, understanding, and support.

When experiencing these moments, honour those raw feelings within you and allow yourself to feel whatever it is for you. Suppressing your emotions or going around the cycle of grief over and over just drags the process out longer. If you have experiences you are grieving or you're struggling with moving forward, find positive ways to support yourself. There is no right or wrong way to do this. If grief is affecting your life in a negative way for a longer period of time than you can manage, reach out, ask for help, and seek support. Educate yourself with information about grief. See a doctor, join a support group, or discuss with a counsellor to help you better understand what you are going through. There is a lot of support available out there. Seeking support is a powerful healing tool in itself. Communicating and sharing our feelings with others during periods of grief is an important part of the process as is feeling acknowledged for what you have shared.

There is light at the end of the tunnel: no matter how dark or long it is, you will get through it. You will look back and realise how far you have come forward from that place. You will enjoy life again! Just put yourself at the top of your priority list, make what you do matter to you, and be patient with yourself.

After all the exploration you just did, we will be working on putting together your plan. This will change your life as much or as little as you want it too: it is up to you! Explore options to turn on your inner light and run with that torch until it is shining so bright, you will connect with your own magic that is within you!

You will also find access to an Australia-wide support resource library on my business page I have put together for you to help you with your research for the support you may want to put into your plan.

CHAPTER 11

EMPOWER YOURSELF AND TAKE ACTION

We are today because of yesterday,

We are tomorrow because of our present choices,

We become in the future, what we believe we can today.

EMPOWER YOURSELF AND TAKE ACTION

If what you are currently doing in your life is not working, or some of what you do works and some doesn't, it might be time to put it behind you. If what you thought was ideal in the past – whether this was love, what you thought was meant to be, or a dream that may not have come to fruition – no longer serves your present circumstances, then it may be time to let it go.

In discarding your old ideals that no longer support you, you will find new ways of living your new life. You will find new goals and new insights. By understanding the experiences that led you to this point with this fresh perspective, new dreams will evolve and lead to new-found gratitude and happiness within.

You have explored the self-help recovery guide and the questions about yourself. Now it is time to dedicate time and energy into yourself. Self-nurture is the key to your new life and the new world that you are creating for yourself.

I healed the infectious bone disease I once had when I was told that a cure was not possible! That alone made me feel mentally and emotionally stronger than I ever had, but not without the painful grieving of the losses of a life I once knew and years of rehabilitation and recovery. But I achieved it, no matter what! You can turn every experience into something greater by your own perception. The way I look at it is: what would I have to give if I didn't live the life I lived? Where would I be now if it wasn't for the life I lived?

Through all my years of trauma, I discovered not only resilience but a powerful source within myself to heal and achieve and keep achieving. You have your own powerful source within you too. *Wake it up!*

Look inside yourself through some of the more challenging experiences. Stop blaming and shaming yourself or others: you are not a victim. You are the creator of your own life! Once you feel this with your heart centre you can achieve anything you set your mind to. Physical or mental limitations, although they may be there to begin with, disappear. The barriers we once faced become easier to problem-solve and we begin looking at our glass "half full," until it is overflowing.

We achieve this by sourcing out all the information and services we may need on what we would like as a part of our future plan. You may need to do some internet research, make a few phone calls to numerous services within your community, or you could consult with a family member or a case manager that can help with sourcing services, support groups, networks, and activities in the community that you may be interested in.

Once you have found what works well, how do we maintain that?

We know that support from those that work with you or care for you is an important part of managing your day-to-day life. But making yourself a priority and really loving yourself is how you maintain this! I know for some it means sitting in front of a mirror and spending four hours doing their hair and make-up to look and feel beautiful, but you can stand in front of a mirror and look beautiful after four minutes of getting out of bed. Men do it all the time! So do I when I am running late for work and still need to feed the animals and poop-scoop the pony's pen, which takes me longer than my hair (lol)!

EMPOWER YOURSELF AND TAKE ACTION

After exploration of all the options we have looked at, I want you to really think about what makes you feel great. If you're not sure, pick a few things out you would like to try and see how it feels. You don't know until you try new things. Once you find what you love, you will feel the reward for yourself! Remember, you deserve to make yourself a priority, so give yourself permission to go to the top of that list. Treat yourself in every way and treat yourself often. Breathe in the healing and indulge every sense that is functioning, including your sixth sense: it is just as real as what we see, what we touch, what we smell, what we hear, what we taste. What we feel inside our heart and spirit is just as important. Here we connect with our intuitions, learning what feels right and good for us.

In the case of those caring for another who may be incapacitated or totally unable to take care of themselves, treat that person with the same care as you would yourself if possible, they will enjoy the experience just as much.

It is really about holistically taking care of every part of ourselves in every way. We have spent much time exploring alternative ways to support your health and wellbeing, and it is now time to put it all together for yourself! Whatever you feel is going to help you get to where you want to be or make the changes that support your life, just do it: this is loving yourself.

MAKING A PLAN

How do we begin planning to attain our goals?

I am going to share with you my *"simple"* and effective way to plan for the future. Take the journey, take action, and make the changes you want to see.

Think about how you would like your life to look, what changes you want to see in your life and just do it: it really is simple! Make this your new mantra.

You are your knight in shining armour! You are a spark in this universe. Ignite your flame, do what it is your heart desires, be the person you want to be, do not let your condition, circumstances, or situation rule you anymore – you rule it! Own yourself, let any limitations be what they are, and work with the ones that are a part of your life.

MY SIMPLE STEPS

- Smile even if the world around you has a frown
- I am powerful: believe in yourself wholeheartedly
- Mirror the reflection of what you want to see
- Pleasure all your senses
- Love and care for yourself: you are number one
- Experience new gratitude for all the positives

IT IS THAT SIMPLE

Throughout my life, all the years I have been journaling, keeping diaries and plans, I have set goals, breaking down those goals into smaller achievable goals to achieve the desired outcome of my long-term goal!

EMPOWER YOURSELF AND TAKE ACTION

Breaking down your goals into smaller goals and setting weekly tasks toward achieving your long-term goal helps you get your head around what you need to do to achieve whatever your desired outcome is.

Once you set the desired goals for the next 12 months, break these down into three monthly goals to better understand what you need to do in the short-term to achieve what you want in the long-term.

Following this, make a weekly plan of tasks you need to do in order to achieve your first three-month goal. I want you to look at planning around *how* you are going to achieve each goal within that three months, *prioritising and diarising*, setting tasks in your diary or calendar to makes things happen. Set up whatever supports are necessary to help you get there and empower yourself with whatever you need. Then take action and begin working towards what you want!

Take a look at two examples I have created of a 12-month goal, beginning with the first three-month goal broken down into weekly tasks.

EXAMPLE ONE
If anxieties, fears, or grief are affecting your life in a negative way for a longer period of time than what would seem "normal," ask for help, seek support, and educate yourself with information about grief: see a doctor, join a support group, or talk to a counsellor to help you better understand what you are going through. It is important to seek help when needed.

12 Month Goal – feel happier and overcome the grief

Three Month Goal – this might begin with regular counselling and learning healthier ways to manage your emotions and put your focus on activities that make you feel happy again

Weekly Tasks – your weekly tasks or activities within your plan to achieve your three-month goal may be to research supports, community services and activities, and write them in your plan. Start making phone-calls, make appointments, attend the appointments weekly, fortnightly, or as often as you can. Also attend the activity weekly that you want to focus on that makes you feel happy – attend it more if you can! If you have no transport, it might be finding community transport that can get you to these appointments and activities. Write it all in your plan.

You will have more of a reason to follow through and get it done if it is in your plan. This is a binding contract to yourself. You are worth the effort it takes to get to the end result.

EXAMPLE TWO

Another example might be that you may struggle with your weight and want to lose a desired amount but diets and plans have not previously worked well. Look at what has worked and hasn't worked before. Look at all the lifestyle factors past and present. Try something new.

12 Month Goal – lose 15 kg

Three Month Goal – stick to a regular exercise routine, see a dietician regularly, eat healthier, and learn to manage unhealthy habits

Weekly Tasks – your weekly tasks to work towards achieving this might be starting with researching local gyms, an appointment with a personal trainer, making a regular exercise plan, booking in to see your doctor, getting a medical care plan put in place to access a dietician at no cost to you, and keeping a diary of where you are at weekly as watching results is a great motivator.

EMPOWER YOURSELF AND TAKE ACTION

Let's plan baby! Let's set goals around taking care of every part of you that is important to you. We'll start by making a plan of what we are going to do and how we are going to get it done. Put it into a binding contract you are going to make to yourself, for yourself and your wellbeing! It is really that *simple*.

It is time to pick up your pen and notepad again or feel free to use the space provided.

Let's start our plan with a checklist of ideas that may apply to you. Remember, you only need add what applies to bettering your life. As we move further into this exercise, jump online, check out the Australia-wide resource library I put together on my Facebook Face of Faith Wellness business page @faceoffaithwellness to help access supports and contacts you may be wanting to add in your plan. If you don't have access to the internet at home, find your nearest library as they offer free internet access, using your own device or their computers.

Here is a list of the other topics we previously covered for you to choose to add into your plan:

- Three main goals
- Educational courses or training on topics you want to learn about
- Declutter
- Self-care
- Nutrition
- Activity, sport, or exercise
- Rest, rejuvenate, recover
- Mindful meditation practise
- Alternate therapies

- Artistic therapy
- Music and sound
- Create a support network of community support services and a case manager that can assist with finding support for your everyday life with personal care, cleaning, gardening, transport, shopping etc.
- Counselling support

This time, reflect back on all the answers to the questions in previous chapters to assess how your feeling, the daily challenges you're facing, and what you would like to be doing differently. Let's then delve deeper into this by covering things that may have even changed since going through those questions. With the time it took to get from there to here you may have been working on some of these things or have some new ideas. If so, that is fantastic!

Now, I just want to say WOW! You are amazing. Don't stop now! Keep going, and you will be feeling happier in no time at all. You will begin to tap into yourself and your own magic.

EMPOWER YOURSELF AND TAKE ACTION

CREATE YOUR CONTRACT

MY PLAN TO IMPROVE MY LIFE THE WAY I WANT IT TO BE

Today's date: _____

Name beautiful you ♥: _____

12-Month Goal:
Begin with three goals you would like to achieve in the next 12 months. Anything that is important to you or that you want for yourself. Additionally, add an activity or interest you would like to be doing!

1. _____
2. _____
3. _____

Activity, exercise, or other interest I would like to engage in:

_____
_____

For each of those goals, break them down into three-monthly goals. These are what you will aim to achieve in three-monthly blocks to reach your 12-month goal. A week-by-week planner and space for reflecting on the first three months of each goal is included as well – you can continue using this same structure to map out and reflect on your following three-month goals.

FACE of FAITH

GOAL 1
0-3 months   Start date _____

_____
_____
_____
_____

Support I would like to put in place to help me achieve these

_____
_____
_____
_____

3-6 months   Start date _____

_____
_____
_____
_____

Supports I would like to put in place to help me achieve these

_____
_____
_____
_____

EMPOWER YOURSELF AND TAKE ACTION

6-9 months   Start Date _____

_____
_____
_____
_____

Supports I would like to put in place to help me achieve these

_____
_____
_____
_____

9-12 months   Start Date _____

_____
_____
_____
_____

Supports I would like to put in place to help me achieve these

_____
_____
_____
_____

WEEKLY PLANNER

Remember SIMPLE steps each week for the first three months to achieve your goal. Write them in below and schedule them in your diary, calendar, or on your to-do list to make these steps, tasks, or activities a priority.

Week 1 _____

_____

How did week 1 go for you?

_____

_____

_____

Week 2 _____

_____

How did week 2 go for you? _____

_____

Week 3 _____

_____

How did week 3 go for you? _____

_____

EMPOWER YOURSELF AND TAKE ACTION

Week 4 _____
_____

How did week 4 go for you? _____
_____

Week 5 _____
_____

How did week 5 go for you? _____
_____

Week 6 _____
_____

How did week 6 go for you? _____
_____

Week 7 _____
_____

How did week 7 go for you? _____
_____

FACE *of* FAITH

Week 8 _____
_____

How did week 8 go for you? _____
_____

Week 9 _____
_____

How did week 9 go for you? _____
_____

Week 10 _____
_____

How did week 10 go for you? _____
_____

Week 11 _____
_____

How did week 11 go for you? _____
_____

EMPOWER YOURSELF AND TAKE ACTION

Week 12 _____
_____

How did week 12 go for you? _____
_____

GOAL 2

0-3 months   Start date _____

_____
_____
_____
_____

Support I would like to put in place to help me achieve these

_____
_____
_____
_____

3-6 months   Start date _____

_____
_____
_____
_____

Supports I would like to put in place to help me achieve these

_____
_____
_____
_____

EMPOWER YOURSELF AND TAKE ACTION

6-9 months   Start Date _____

_____
_____
_____
_____

Supports I would like to put in place to help me achieve these

_____
_____
_____
_____

9-12 months   Start Date _____

_____
_____
_____
_____

Supports I would like to put in place to help me achieve these

_____
_____
_____
_____

WEEKLY PLANNER

Remember SIMPLE steps each week for the first three months to achieve your goal. Write them in below and schedule them in your diary, calendar, or on your to-do list to make these steps, tasks, or activities a priority.

Week 1 _____
_____

How did week 1 go for you?
_____
_____
_____

Week 2 _____
_____

How did week 2 go for you? _____
_____

Week 3 _____
_____

How did week 3 go for you? _____
_____

EMPOWER YOURSELF AND TAKE ACTION

Week 4 _____
_____

How did week 4 go for you? _____
_____

Week 5 _____
_____

How did week 5 go for you? _____
_____

Week 6 _____
_____

How did week 6 go for you? _____
_____

Week 7 _____
_____

How did week 7 go for you? _____
_____

FACE of FAITH

Week 8 _____
_____

How did week 8 go for you? _____
_____

Week 9 _____
_____

How did week 9 go for you? _____
_____

Week 10 _____
_____

How did week 10 go for you? _____
_____

Week 11 _____
_____

How did week 11 go for you? _____
_____

EMPOWER YOURSELF AND TAKE ACTION

Week 12 _____
_____

How did week 12 go for you? _____
_____

FACE of FAITH

GOAL 3
0-3 months   Start date _____

_____
_____
_____
_____

Support I would like to put in place to help me achieve these
_____
_____
_____
_____

3-6 months   Start date _____

_____
_____
_____
_____

Supports I would like to put in place to help me achieve these
_____
_____
_____
_____

EMPOWER YOURSELF AND TAKE ACTION

6-9 months   Start Date _____

_____
_____
_____
_____

Supports I would like to put in place to help me achieve these

_____
_____
_____
_____

9-12 months   Start Date _____

_____
_____
_____
_____

Supports I would like to put in place to help me achieve these

_____
_____
_____
_____

FACE of FAITH

WEEKLY PLANNER

Remember SIMPLE steps each week for the first three months to achieve your goal. Write them in below and schedule them in your diary, calendar, or on your to-do list to make these steps, tasks, or activities a priority.

Week 1 _____

_____

How did week 1 go for you?

_____
_____
_____

Week 2 _____

_____

How did week 2 go for you? _____

_____

Week 3 _____

_____

How did week 3 go for you? _____

_____

EMPOWER YOURSELF AND TAKE ACTION

Week 4 _____
_____

How did week 4 go for you? _____
_____

Week 5 _____
_____

How did week 5 go for you? _____
_____

Week 6 _____
_____

How did week 6 go for you? _____
_____

Week 7 _____
_____

How did week 7 go for you? _____
_____

FACE *of* FAITH

Week 8 _____
_____

How did week 8 go for you? _____
_____

Week 9 _____
_____

How did week 9 go for you? _____
_____

Week 10 _____
_____

How did week 10 go for you? _____
_____

Week 11 _____
_____

How did week 11 go for you? _____
_____

EMPOWER YOURSELF AND TAKE ACTION

Week 12 _____
_____

How did week 12 go for you? _____
_____

Names and contact details of community supports, services, and family/friends that I can call on to assist me in achieving my goals:

1. _____
2. _____
3. _____
4. _____
5. _____
6. _____

During the next 12 months, while executing your plan, here are some things that we have looked at that you can do for yourself to keep your motivation intact.

Stay connected with close family and friends. Just spending time with them can help you feel connected, openly communicate how you're feeling, and what you are doing. Keep a diary or use this book to take notes each day on how you're travelling with the tasks you set for yourself. Writing helps us reflect and empty the mind so that you don't need to use your energy thinking about it.

Take "care" of yourself, get the rest and/or sleep you need, eat foods that nourish your body, and take time out as often as you need.

ENERGY VERSUS EFFORT

If you're post-surgery and your goal is to complete some form of rehabilitation or physio program, then rebuilding your physical and mental strength from whatever your situation is can be exhausting, even overwhelming. Just getting out of bed and showering can be exhausting. I know as I have been there many times through recoveries, and planning. It felt impossible to achieve the simplest of tasks I set for myself. At times, it can be difficult to get out of bed when you are unwell, suffer chronic pain, are going through treatment, recovering from an injury, live with a permanent condition, or feel bogged down with life and its day-to-day stuff – let alone stay motivated!

Each and every time you feel this way, I want you to remind yourself that the *energy* you will create within you and the benefits you will gain, will far outweigh the *effort* you put in to *work toward the desired outcome!*

Remember the purpose: go back to *why* you are doing what you are doing. Have a look over your first lot of questions and answers. What do you want out of this? Are you feeling satisfied? Are you settling for comfortable or less than comfortable? What works for you? You already know what does not work and how that feels!

Be kind to yourself, but being kind does not mean doing nothing – that is not taking care of yourself at all! Loving yourself is taking even the smallest of steps forward: completing ten or 20 minutes of physio exercise a day, going for a walk, journaling, or doing whatever daily task or activity you have set for yourself that supports your plan to achieve your goal.

I got out of bed every day and kept at it. Even the smallest task is an achievement. Be just as appreciative and proud of yourself for those

EMPOWER YOURSELF AND TAKE ACTION

and I assure you, no matter what, you will be ticking off completed tasks at the end of every week. You will find *your* sweet spot, your happiness, and *your* magic.

Step out of your comfort zone. After all you have been through; you owe it to yourself!

CHAPTER 12
MIND DYSPLASIA TO MINDFULNESS

The world we reside upon is far from perfection

The way we see it is in our perception

Look for heart-warming colours from our daytime sun

Witness fairies and angels dance having fun

Goddesses of our garden's light

Your wings sparkle glistening bright

Rainbow colours of velvety lusciousness

Closely connected a warm lustrousness.

MIND DYSPLASIA TO MINDFULNESS

Did you have a go at filling in your answers to the questions to get a feel for where you are at, what changes you might be looking at, and what you want for yourself? How did you go with your contract to yourself? Did you make a plan for how you are going to achieve what changes and goals you want for your life? If so, fantastic! I am so happy for you that you have engaged and focused on yourself all the way.

For those who haven't, or feel a little stuck on some parts, don't worry: just remember the answers you are seeking are somewhere within you! If you want to feel a great happiness inside your heart and are considering making changes to your life, wake up those inner stirrings that have been probing you along the way. The best part is, you get to make it up as you go along. It is your plan to make up, your contract to make with yourself. It is your dream, it is *YOUR LIFE!*

From this moment, it is your life: you decide the thoughts you want to think, the goals you want to achieve, the clothes you want to wear, the choices you make, and how your life is going to be lived. Any life experience, trauma, or condition you have does NOT decide anymore – you do! We know the past and its limitations. We may have limits and boundaries to work within but that is not going to stop us from being the best we can be and living a productive and happy life.

Remember to shift the focus by putting your attention towards creating the life you want to be living and what you do want for yourself. Take the focus completely away from what you don't want in your life anymore.

Energy flows where attention goes.

Don't worry if you have times where you lose yourself in something; it is all a part of growing. Just becoming aware of it and recognising when another person or experience disrupts your inner calm brings you halfway back to yourself already.

We all have moments of what I call mind dysplasia: we are human. Next time it happens, bring your focus back to your breath, calm your breath, and lengthen and deepen your breathing. Try this just now. Take a few deep, slow breaths.

This type of breathing sends the message to our nervous system that we are safe and can relax, switching off those chemicals that release during stress. This will calm your mind, even if it just for a brief period. Here, you will connect with you!

That's where I found the answers to questions I had been asking for so long, and you will too. Here is where you will find and see the magic in any trauma, life experience, and in yourself.

We have a choice: a choice to make changes. When you plant a seed, give it water, fertiliser, food, and light, it grows, just as we do. We physically grow from the day of our conception and learn from everything that we are taught and everything that happens to us along the way. If you think negative or self-sabotaging thoughts (and keep on thinking them), you are feeding them because they are growing too. If we feed those parts of ourselves that we want to develop by focusing on the changes we want to make, they will grow and manifest into what we want! If you believe you deserve the best out of life and strive for the best, you will vibrate at that frequency and you will receive the best.

If you believe negative things about yourself or your circumstances, there will always be a pile of it in front of you in the form of people, events, and experiences that reflect what we believe about ourselves! Remember our vibrational field is always drawing experiences to us that we can learn and grow from.

MINDFULNESS

Learning about mindfulness begins with the mind. It involves observing what you are feeling and thinking about and coming back into your body and into the present moment, connecting to what you are doing right now. Right now, I am typing and all my awareness is focused on what I want to say. Right now, you are reading, so that is where your awareness only needs to be at this moment.

When you find yourself getting wound up, allow any feelings to rise in the body, acknowledge them, and breathe through those feelings. Take a few big deep breaths and feel yourself begin to relax.

Here, we are going to look at some mindful strategies that support a connection to yourself.

Positive affirmations are a powerful tool. This involves using words and statements to assist in changing negative behaviours, thought patterns, and any negative beliefs you may have about yourself into more positive beliefs and behaviours. These can help you release any thoughts or beliefs that keep us stuck, and build your confidence in yourself, help keep you focused on your intentions and what you want for yourself. Here, you are encouraging every cell in your body, including your brain, to listen and connect!

I like to use the empowering intent of "I am" at the beginning of my positive affirmations to feel the change I want to make as though it has already happened. Really affirm these statements to yourself and believe them – believe in you!

You can write your own statements the way you want. Make your own affirmations list or pick some of the following I have written as examples and pin them up somewhere you can see them. Read them out loud every day. Make them your mantra to yourself.

- I am beautiful inside and out
- I am healthy and feeling fantastic
- I am fit and have a healthy body
- I am happy
- I am wonderful
- I am awesome
- I am magical
- I am healed
- I am loving and deserve love
- I am brave
- I am unstoppable
- I am strong
- I am enough
- I am worthy
- I am self-empowered
- I am abundant
- I am happy
- I am free
- I am resilient
- I love myself for all that I am
- I release all guilt completely
- I release all fear completely
- Abundance flows in all areas of my life

MIND DYSPLASIA TO MINDFULNESS

FACE OF FAITH WELLNESS MEDITATION

Here is a guided healing meditation I wrote for you. You can read it to yourself whilst listening to relaxation music. This takes up to ten minutes. Take time out of your day or night to relax your mind and body.

Take three big beautiful deep breaths in, filling the deepest part of your lungs with air

Feel your belly expand as you breathe in

Breathing gently and slowly

If you notice any worrisome thoughts

Allow them to drift away from the space you are in now

Stay connected to your breath, gently breathing in

Gently breathing out through any thoughts that arise

Loving breath in, loving breath out

Slowing down the breath, find your body's own natural breathing rhythm

If you notice any pain or tension you may be carrying

Bring your attention back to your breath, breathing gently and lovingly through any pain

FACE of FAITH

Visualise a soft pink light

Breathe this soft pink light in through your mouth

Spreading gently throughout your face, completely relaxing

All the muscles in and around your face, your skull, your brain

Spreading this light down into your neck, your shoulders

Lovingly breathe this soft pink glow into the depth of your lungs

Visualise this pink glow filling your entire body, entering your arms

Your hands and fingers, breathing into all your nerves, muscles, and skin

Allowing this soft pink light to permeate through your lungs

As you gently breathe it into your stomach, your hips, and down into your legs

Your knees, and through to your feet and your toes

With each breath, spread this soft pink light as it sweeps through your entire body

Lovingly breathing in and gently breathing out

Bring yourself back to the position you are in

Come back into your awareness with your breath

MIND DYSPLASIA TO MINDFULNESS

Move your hands and feet, then move your whole body

And notice how your entire body feels right now.

VIBRATIONAL ENERGIES THROUGH CHAKRAS AND CRYSTALS

There are minor and major energy centres throughout the body. This knowledge has been taught around the world from ancient documentation. Here, we are briefly looking at the seven main energy centres.

During meditation, you can use these energy centres with the use of the Earth's crystals to enhance the vibrational quality of your meditation and assist in healing. There are a few crystals that can be used to bring balance to each chakra. If they are blocked or over-activated, this can bring imbalance to our lives.

Seven Main Chakra Energy Systems

Crown chakra, in balance, connects us to our compassion, spiritual connection, self-awareness, and fulfilment. It is located at the top of the crown. Crystals that assist this chakra are clear quartz and sugilite.

Brow or third eye chakra, in balance, connects us to our intuition, wisdom, and charisma. It is located between your brow. Crystals that assist this chakra are amethyst and lapis lazuli.

Throat chakra, in balance, connects us to our effective communication, feelings of self-worth, and self-confidence. It is located at your throat centre. Crystals that assist this chakra are turquoise and aquamarine.

Heart chakra, in balance, connects us to our unconditional love, self-nurture, and happiness. It is located at the centre of your chest. Crystals that assist this chakra are rose quartz and jade.

Solar plexus chakra, in balance, connects us to our strength, self-respect, and self-connectedness. It is located just above your navel area. Crystals that assist this chakra are citrine and jasper.

Sacral chakra, in balance, connects us to our emotions, creativity, and pleasures. It is located just above your sacrum. Crystals that assist here are carnelian and moonstone.

Base or root chakra, in balance, connects us to our sense of security, self-care, grounding. It is located at the base of spine. Crystals that assist here are garnet and smoky quartz.

Here is a diagram to show the locations of chakras and where you can place your crystals during a meditation.

MIND DYSPLASIA TO MINDFULNESS

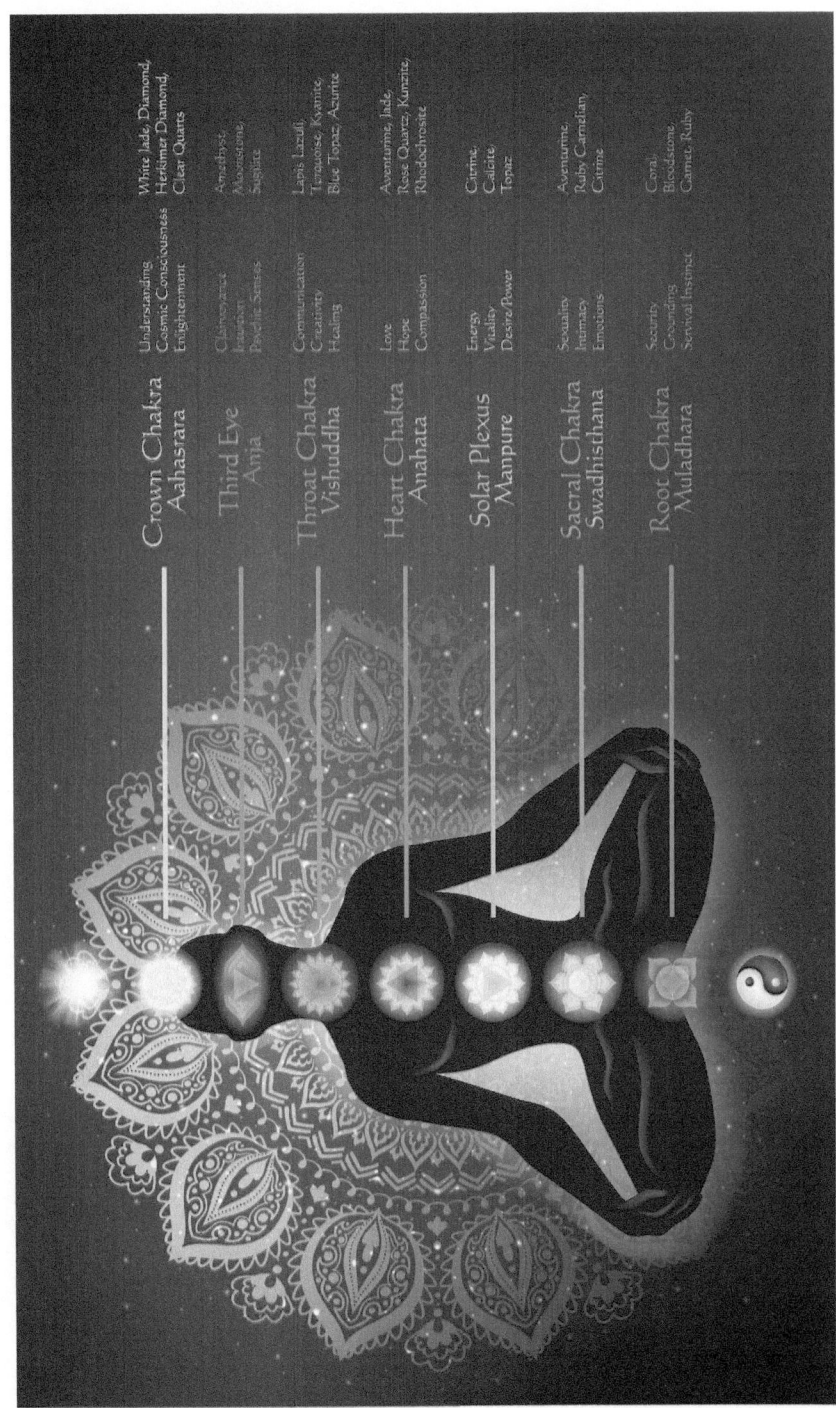

FIND YOUR MAGIC THROUGH TRAUMA

Overcome the past. The past is over and done. It cannot be erased. The present is all we need to be focusing on: what we are doing today toward creating our happiness for tomorrow, which becomes our present when we wake up in the morning. We can only work through our challenges if we are present in dealing with them.

The serenity prayer reminds me when I am faced with a situation that is out of my control: "to accept the things I cannot change, the courage to change the things I can, and the wisdom to know the difference."

Everything happens for a reason. There is a purpose for the experiences we go through. We don't always know why or how. But I do know that when you connect with this and realise we are a part of this entire universe and the creation of it all, we begin to ask questions about the bigger picture of our lives and why things happen the way they do. The answers you want to your current situations, your illness, injury, disability, and the changes you want to make, are all inside you!

Have you ever asked, "Why me? Why this?" Well, I have the answer to that, but with another question: why not? Why not use your experience to better your life, show the way for others, to help others, or to make a difference? You have nothing to lose, only great change to be gained.

Look for the gifts, wisdom, courage, connections, resilience, love, generosity, gratitude, and lessons learnt in any experience, and share it. You will suddenly see the world you live in as a different place to how you once perceived it.

I kept all my paperwork, songs, poems, journals, and medical files stored in folders, in my computer, and in my heart for so long, keeping it there as though it was some valuable jewel that must be kept under lock and key. There was no real purpose for the contents of my life to stay filed and locked inside my heart. I made the empowering decision to open the door to my files and share my life to empower each of you with my own experiences and everything I learnt along the way.

This has become my purpose: to share with you all the magic I discovered, in the hope of giving you hope and knowledge that with any condition, injury, illness, trauma, loss, or pain, with support you will find resilience and the gift of strength to face life's challenges!

Be the face of faith for others. Show that you "can" no matter what.

ABOUT THE AUTHOR

Shelley Maree grew up in various places and properties throughout Victoria, training and competing with long distance endurance horses. She was shifted from pillar to post, and exposed to motorcycle club life and violence. Later, she moved around multiple states and travelled the Australian countryside.

Shelley has studied among various educational institutions, gaining multiple certifications and qualifications in fitness and health, alternative healing and spiritual energetic practises, social and community services, community services work, with extensive disability and mental health training. She has worked among the field of the tattoo art industry, managing businesses, aged care, and is currently working on the ground level as a disability and mental health worker, supporting clients with living skills training, achieving their goals, their wellbeing, and hands-on care work!

Shelley currently lives in Canberra, Australia, enjoying yoga, body balance, daily meditation practise and writing. Her interests include creating all kinds of things and weekends away fishing!

Her plan is to offer further support to others on their healing journeys and further her training and practise in yin yoga, promoting health and wellbeing after trauma, and add yin yoga workshops as an extension to her programs. The long-term dream is to set up a cabin-style retreat in a bush setting on a property of her own, offering weekend wellness retreats.

Shelley is not aligned with any one religion, but lives a contemporary [existing now] lifestyle. Shelley is an empowering force behind supporting personal and spiritual growth and healing through all of life's experiences that changes how we perceive our inner and outer world.

ACKNOWLEDGEMENTS

You have come as far as reading this entire book. It makes me feel proud and happy that my journey has found its way into your heart. While you are almost at the end, it is the beginning of a new chapter for you!

Thank you for staying with me. You have done yourself a huge favour! You have been kind to you. I want you to continue this greatness you are doing for yourself. Show yourself love like there is no tomorrow. Stay focused on your goals and what you want. Support yourself in every way. You are worth it!

I have empowered you with everything you need to answer your own questions, grow your self-awareness, and make choices that improve your life in every way, bringing you back home.

I have exposed parts of the road I have travelled and where I have been in the hope that this knowledge and experience brings you understanding, paving the way to empower and own yourself, make positive choices that support your way to healing, to health, to happiness, and to ultimately finding your own magic!

FACE *of* FAITH

No matter what your circumstances are and no matter what journey you are on – for those working in a health or medical profession, across the community sector, or supporting people as a care giver – you can all benefit from this content. We all need support and care. It plays a huge part in people's lives. I am hopeful in a shift in attitudes and holistic approaches toward short- and long-term rehabilitation and recovery management plans by seeing things from the inspirational place within us all.

We are not just our title, a patient, a client, a number: we are human and we feel deeply about our journeys. The environment and society around us impact greatly on our healing and our lives. Be kind to yourself through it all and share your journey with others. You never know who might be inspired and find their magic in that. Keep at what is working well for you to find your sweet spot, the magic that is YOU.

Thank you for purchasing this book, supporting my journey, and most of all for working on a new and improved you. Feel free to contact us and share how the broken pieces of your past are turning into a magical life!

BE YOURSELF OWN YOURSELF LOVE YOURSELF

THREE BONUS OFFERS

We have three bonus offers to share with you for continued support to overcome your challenges and live your happiest life!

Go to my Facebook business page, Face of Faith Wellness @faceoffaithwellness. Here, you will see links to our contact email address to contact us for these offers. On this page, there is also a link to our Face of Faith Wellness Facebook group. Click join if you would like to join our group. This is a safe space where you can network with us and other readers and share your experience of reading and working through *Face of Faith* or your own journey.

OFFER 1
I have created an Australia-wide resource library and Service Provider Directory for you to search up any supports you may be able to use as a starting point to put into your plan. This is to assist you to search for supports you may require when working towards achieving your goals and what you want for yourself so you can live life in the way you want to be living.

OFFER 2

A Face of Faith Wellness self-loving meditation, supporting relaxation, and inner calm through the breath, written and audio by Shelley Maree.

OFFER 3

A low-cost, full-day Face Of Faith Wellness Workshop, offering creative mentoring and holistic tools to assist you in overcoming your day-to-day challenges, help you make a plan toward your goals, and learn to support yourself to achieve them, all while we support you to live your happiest life and find your magic!

NOTES

FACE *of* **FAITH**

NOTES

www.ingramcontent.com/pod-product-compliance
Lightning Source LLC
Chambersburg PA
CBHW021832110526
R18278200001B/R182782PG44588CBX00005B/5